Jewish Lives Project.
Sport

British Library cataloguing-in-Publication Data
A catalogue record for this book is available from
the British Library

ISBN 978-1-9998246-5-5

Jewish Museum London
Raymond Burton House
Albert Street, Camden Town
London NW1 7NB
Telephone: 020 7284 7384

Jacket: the illustration of Rosalind Franklin was created
especially for this book series by Laurie Rosenwald.

Cover: the cover pattern is reproduced from selected
biography images from within the book.

Published by the Jewish Museum, London, England
Designed by Webb & Webb Design Limited, London, England
Printed and bound in the U.K.

Opposite "Nero", Harry Blacker was a Jewish cartoonist and poster designer known as Nero. Football is a recurring subject in his Jewish themed cartoons, probing the identity of a community torn between tradition and assimilation.

Mariv will be at six o'clock tonight and Match of the Day at ten on BBC1

"If you won't let me watch Chelsea next Saturday, I'm going to become a rabbi instead of a brain surgeon."

Harry "Nero" Blacker

Acknowledgements

This book would not have been possible without the generosity and financial support of the Kirsh Charitable Foundation, and the creative vision of Lord Young. The Jewish Museum London would also like to thank the following individuals who have significantly contributed to the content of Jewish Lives Project. Sport: Nathan Abrams, Jonathan Bennett, Sacha Bennett, David Bownes, Janette Dalley, Katy Ferguson, Langley Fisher, Marina Fiorato, Jacqui Lewis, John Lewis, Ian Lillicrapp, Anna Lloyd, Rosalyn Livshin, Abigail Morris, Kathrin Pieren, Joanne Rosenthal, Laurie Rosenwald, William Rubinstein, Elizabeth Selby, Sara Semic, Brian and James Webb and Wynn Wheldon

Contents

Preface

Rt Hon Lord Young of Graffham, CH.
Chairman of the Jewish Museum London

This is the sixth and final volume in the Jewish Lives project. Previous volumes have covered Art, Science, Commerce, Public Service, Thought and now Sport. These volumes, taken as a whole, cover the full range of the interests of the Jewish community in the United Kingdom but is confined to those members of our community no longer with us. As a result, this volume looks back to an earlier generation, a generation in many cases of immigrants or the children of immigrants and demonstrates how they took advantage of opportunities that had long been denied their fathers. The fact that this is the thinnest volume of the series cannot be denied, but in decades to come, when a new volume will be published, the balance would have changed and would be considerably more substantial.

The full range of interests of our community, and their contribution can be seen on our website (www.JewishLivesProject.com) which has over two thousand entries and covers those contributing today as well in the past and shows how our community now plays a more than full part in the life of the country.

A cursory look at this book would confirm that we have a special affinity for chess and the number of Jewish grandmasters and tournament winners are legion. Perhaps all the centuries of isolation in ghettos and studying the Talmud have created a mindset and an ability to memorise the countless openings and gambits so essential to chess. It was Jacques Mieses, a member of

Visit the website:
www.JewishLivesProject.com

our community, who in 1950 became the first British player to be recognised as a grandmaster by the World Chess Federation.

If there is a theme that runs through this book it is how new immigrants, arriving in a strange country, often find that the quickest route to acceptance in society lies through sport.

The first members of the Jewish community to gain public acceptance were some of the early boxers epitomised by Daniel Mendoza, known as "the Fighting Jew", the first Jewish sporting celebrity who was also the first Jew to be presented to King George III. In the last century football presented the best opportunity for advancement and this book outlines the histories of some of the early players and the management as football grew to become the global game of today.

Even cricket was not immune from our community and the name of Fred Trueman appears this book who only discovered his Jewish origins after his playing days were over. In athletics anyone who has seen the film Chariots of Fire will know of Harold Abrahams but it was his elder brother Sidney (Solly) Abrahams who competed in the 1912 Stockholm Olympics. Their father was an immigrant.

I cannot finish without thanking Natie Kirsh and the Kirsh Foundation who have not only enabled these books to be published but have also allowed us to produce a series of exhibitions that shows in convincing detail how our community has contributed to the life of the nation.

Opposite Fred Trueman in action during a County match against Somerset, 1965.

CENTENARY YEAR

1863 - 1963

4

YOUTH INTERNATIONAL

1

9

10

11

2

P9211

8

Visit the museum:
Jewish Museum London
Raymond Burton House
Albert Street, Camden Town
London NW1 7NB

5

1. England schoolboy cap and photograph

Pleat won this international cap representing England at schoolboy level.

1960

2. Nottingham Forest photograph

Pleat's senior playing career began at his local club, Nottingham Forest.

c. 1962

5 & 6. England youth international cap and shirt

Whilst at Nottingham Forest, Pleat played for the England youth team.

1963

3. In action for Luton Town

Pleat moved to Luton Town from Nottingham Forest in 1964.

Mid 1960s

4. Representing Britain

Pleat represented Britain at the Maccabiah games in Israel winning gold, the first time playing for Nottingham Forest.

1965

7. Photograph of Pleat with other well known Tottenham figures

2008

9. Champion for Peace

After Peterborough, Pleat retired as a player and moved on to management.

8. Representative match medal

Pleat won this medal managing an English representative team in a game against the Italian League.

1985

As manager, Pleat took Luton Town to the First Division, ending the 1971/72 season on Division Two with record points.

10. FA Cup Final medal

In the 1986/7 season, as manager of Tottenham Hotspur, Pleat put into practice a 4–5–1 formation which was progressive for its time. The team finished third in the league, reaching the semi-finals of the League Cup and the FA Cup Final.

1987

11. Photograph of Pleat winning Sportsman of the Year

As manager in the 1980s, Pleat transformed Luton Town into a major club in English football. In 2012 he was inducted into the League Managers Association Hall of Fame.

1986

Introduction

Abigail Morris

Director, Jewish Museum London

This is the last, and perhaps least obvious, book in our *Jewish Lives* series which celebrates the contribution Jews have made to Britain. Other titles, celebrating Jews as artists, scientists, thinkers, business people and philanthropists have been met with sagacious nods. But Jews as *sporting* heroes? It's certainly not a familiar narrative in Britain, where Jews continue to be associated with cerebral, rather than physical, pursuits.

And though this volume may be slightly slimmer and trimmer than the others I think it's worth quoting one of our most famous rabbis, the medievalist Maimonides who lived in Spain and then in Egypt and wrote books that are still considered core texts and are widely studied today. He was also a respected doctor as in those days rabbis and rabbinic study were part-time and scholars had 'day jobs' too.

Maimonides made many deep, serious, and complicated pronouncements about God, belief, charity and Judaism. But he also told us to exercise. He said we should do at least 30 minutes three times a week to keep both our minds and bodies fit. This is pretty much in line with current medical advice.

11

To finish, a few explanations regarding the selection of portraits in this book. To return to that most complicated of questions: Who is a Jew? The question has been answered in many different ways across time and place. The Jewish Museum have decided on a broad and inclusive definition. We include the children of Jewish parents – not just Jewish mothers. Being Jewish is a mix of inheritance, culture and religion. You can be an atheist Jew who practises or not. You can be born a Jew or convert to Judaism. You can be deeply religious and non-practising. It can be tribal, cultural, religious or nationalistic. In cases where people are born Jewish but disassociate, we have included them but stated that they didn't consider themselves Jewish.

Another definition we wrestled with is the question of who is British. Some on our list were born here, and some settled here. Some worked here for decades, some for a brief but significant period of their career, and it is noticeable how many of them were émigrés who found safe haven in the UK. Finally, the book series only features people who are no longer with us.

So enjoy this book about Jews and sport, read the others in the series too if you haven't, but don't forget to follow the great rabbi's advice and exercise your body sometimes as well as your brain!

If you want to find out about thousands of other British Jews past and present and their contributions to British society, visit www.JewishLivesProject.com

Opposite Maccabiah Games, the British athletes parading in the stadium at the 2nd Maccabiah Games opening ceremony in 1935

"Probably the greatest fighter to come out of Britain."

Mike Tyson

Famous Jewish Sports Legends

Boxing News called Ted "Kid" Lewis "pound for pound the greatest fighting machine England has produced". Lewis fought close to 300 matches and held a world record nine titles at three different weights.

Ted "Kid" Lewis, born Gershon Mendeloff, Lewis is often ranked among the all-time greats. His success in America made him an international celebrity. He was also a close friend of Charlie Chaplin, seen here sparring with Lewis.

Famous Jewish Sports Legends

Nathan Abrams

Professor of Film Studies, Bangor University

Clearly Judaism has historically frowned upon sports and, even more so, female participation in it. A clue can be found in the classic movie *Airplane* when a passenger asks for something "light" to read and is presented with the leaflet, *Famous Jewish Sports Legends*.

It has long been a staple of Jewish humour that Jews do not do sports. That's because Jews were perceived as weak, frail, small, non-athletic, urban (ghetto) businessmen. They are marked by their intelligence, cunning quick wit and verbal rather than physical skills. They have more brains than brawn.

There is some truth to this. Judaism has rarely placed an emphasis on athleticism. Indeed, the opposite has been the case; in ancient times sport, as it then existed, clashed with Judaism's system of belief and values. The Greeks combined physical with spiritual activity, using sport, the stadium and the gymnasium, the Olympics, as a sacred, symbolic and religious rite to honour the gods. For Jews who participated in such sports, therefore, it was a means to reject their religious and ethnic origins to assimilate and integrate into the Hellenised Greco-Roman world. In exile, Judaism emphasised the importance of observance of God's commandments (mitzvot) over all other activities, although the rabbis encouraged Jews to look after their bodies and maintain their physical fitness to be better able to fulfil the mitzvot correctly.

Ancient Israel may have been an agricultural society, the rituals of which were rooted in the rhythms of nature, but in the aftermath of the destruction of the Second Temple in 70 CE, Jews swapped terrain for text, becoming the "People of the Book" and finding their homeland in the Torah rather than in physical nature. Life itself was perceived as a text. This rebirth entailed de-emphasising physical practice (pilgrimage, Temple sacrifice), which was rejected in favour of mental labour (prayer, study, thought). This non-athletic bookishness and textuality had the side effect of producing a Jewish anti-natural ethic.

During the medieval period, in the diaspora, Jewish involvement in sports and recreational pastimes became a moot point as Jews were denied these opportunities, but two intertwined ideas grew to squeeze out even the notion of Jewish athleticism. The first was the stereotype of the western Jew of the diaspora as unnatural, that he (and I use the gender pronoun deliberately here because it is clear that women are significantly under-represented) does not belong in nature, the precise place where physical, sporting and recreational activity took place.

The issue was compounded from the 10th century onwards when Jews became an urban people. Both medieval Islam and Christianity denied Jews access to land ownership and cultivation. Instead of agriculture, Jews concentrated on commerce, trade and finance, all of which had the added benefit of enabling them to survive frequent expulsions and rapidly adapt to new social conditions.

Physical, martial and bodily virtues, which flowered in nature, were rejected in favour of a scholarliness that thrived indoors. Jews, denied the right to bear arms, ride horses, duel, joust or arch competitively, in return rejected the competitive drive ethos of what they disparagingly called goyim naches; that is literally pleasure for the gentiles, but which refers to those characteristics that in European culture have defined a man as manly: physical strength, martial activity and aggressiveness. Since the word goy is related to geviyah (Hebrew for body), the word goyim can also be interpreted to mean bodily, thus diaspora Jews rejected manly bodily pursuits, namely fighting, duelling, wrestling, hunting and sports.

Consequently, for centuries thereafter, Jewish physiognomy and physiology have tenaciously been intertwined with notions of unmanly passivity, weakness, hysteria and pathology, all bred by the lack of outdoor and healthy activity. Jewish legs and feet were characterised as un-athletic and unsuited to both sport and combat. In part, Jews had their role to play in this because they valorised timidity, meekness, physical frailty and gentleness, privileging the pale scholarly Jew who studied indoors, excluded from labour and warfare.

But things began to change in more recent centuries. In Britain, in the late 18th and then again in the early 20th centuries, Jewish boxers arose. Champion Jewish prizefighters included Daniel Mendoza, "Dutch Sam" Elias, Barney Aaron, Aschel Joseph, Sid Burns, Matthew Wells, Ted "Kid" Lewis and Jack "Kid" Berg.

This was because sports provided Jewish youngsters with a way to prove their athletic prowess and shoot down traditional stereotypes of Jews as physically weak, effete, intellectual, frail and bookish.

What is more, in Britain between 1874 and 1914, sport and physical recreation played a key role in the "Anglicisation" of the children of the thousands of eastern European Jewish immigrants who permanently settled in London, as English Jews enthusiastically mimicked the codes of Muscular Christianity as an assimilatory strategy. Their objective was to produce "Englishmen of the Mosaic Persuasion". The first initiative to be set up was the Jewish Working Men's Club and Institute in 1874, which introduced initially athletics and drill, followed by cycling, football and cricket, among Jews. A

Samuel Elias, better known as "Dutch Sam".

Spurs, antisemitic chants have directed at the club and its supporters by rival fans since the 1960s.

new network of youth clubs and social and sporting organisations
was established in the belief that the introduction and promotion
of British sport among the "alien" children was an effective means
of "Anglicisation". Accomplishment in physically demanding sports
was perceived to be the ideal answer to accusations surrounding the
immigrant Jewish physique and its "negative" effect on the British
racial "stock". At the same time, it was felt, the English values of
sportsmanship, fair play and teamwork could be instilled.

Middle-class English sports especially functioned as assimilatory
devices. They literally afforded the opportunity to "whiten up", to
pass as white both literally and figuratively, in that many middle and
upper-class sports demanded the wearing of white attire (running,
tennis, cricket; the English football and rugby teams play in white). It
is probably no coincidence that the team labelled the most "Jewish"
in England, Tottenham Hotspur (est. 1882), are also known as the
"Lily-whites" - because of their adoption of a home kit of white shirt
and blue shorts at the end of the 19th century.

But sport produced a tension between being a good Englishman
and being a good Jew. Sections within the Jewish community soon
began to fear that the focus on physical recreation was undermining
traditional Jewish culture and contributing to a "drift" towards
religious indifference and apostasy. It did not help that so many
sports or sports practice took place on a Saturday. A choice had to
be made: sporting prowess or observing the Sabbath.

Sport may have been conceived as a means to counter anti-
Jewish prejudice, but antisemitism was undoubtedly experienced
in the heated fervour of sporting battle. This may amount to
whispered asides, sledging or racist chanting from the stands, such
as the persistence of the term "Yiddo" in reference to Spurs. In this
context, is it any coincidence that those sports at which Jews tend

to excel – boxing, table tennis, fencing, swimming and chess – take place indoors, away from nature and from bigots? As this list shows, with the exception of boxing, they tend also towards the bourgeois.

To refer back to the opening joke, Jews themselves have been guilty of failing to acknowledge Jewish sporting prowess. While novelist Howard Jacobson might have written a paean to table tennis in his novel *The Mighty Walzer*, contrast this to his debut novel *Coming from Behind*, in which he averred, "In the highly improbable event of his being asked to nominate the one most un-Jewish thing he could think of, Sefton Goldberg would have been hard pressed to decide between Nature […] and football". In one sentence, he compounds all the stereotypes of Jewish anti-naturalistic un-athleticism.

And where are the films and books about Jewish boxers, Jewish fly fishermen, Jewish cricketers, Jewish footballers, Jewish wrestlers, Jewish jockeys and even Jewish motor-car racers? Their feats are not celebrated. If we know about one famous Jewish sportsman, it's because non-Jews made a film about him – Harold Abrahams in *Chariots of Fire*. And therein lies the explanation.

Harold Abrahams (Ben Cross) and Lord Burghley (Nigel Havers) challenge for the Great Court Run – a dash around the main quad of Trinity College, Cambridge, within the time it takes the clock to strike 12. From the 1981 film *Chariots of Fire*.

"…not Mr. Table Tennis only,
but Mr. Sportsman."

Ivor Montagu

Biographies A – C

Winner of seven World Championships, Richard Bergmann was regarded as such a great sportsman that the Richard Bergmann Fair Play Trophy is still awarded at the ITTF World Table Tennis Championships.

"Young" Barney Aaron

The first Jew to win an
American ring championship
1836–1907

"Young" Barney Aaron was born
in London. His father, Barney
Aaron, was a successful bare-
knuckle boxer in the early 1800s.
Nicknamed the "Star of the
East", the elder Barney Aaron
is credited with helping Jews' social standing in London as a result
of his success. "Young" Barney Aaron moved to the United States
in 1855. A year later he launched his bare-knuckle boxing career.
Fighting under London Prize Ring Rules, Aaron's matches were scored
according to the number of rounds within a match. His first match
was against Robinson on Rikers Island in a match that lasted 80
rounds and nearly two and a half hours. Aaron emerged victorious. In
1857 Aaron was the first Jew to win an American ring championship
when he defeated lightweight boxer Johnny Moenghan in Providence.
He made headlines again in 1874 when he rescued the Reverend
Henry Thorpe from two pickpockets in New York. He felled the two
thieves and returned Thorpe's gold watch. After a successful career,
Aaron became a referee and opened a boxing gym in New York. He
was inducted into the International Boxing Hall of Fame in 2007.

Gerald Abrahams
Liverpool lawyer who defeated
a Soviet Grandmaster
1907–1980

Gerald Abrahams was born
in Liverpool, England. He
studied politics, philosophy
and economics at Wadham
College, Oxford. In 1931 he
was called to the Bar at Gray's
Inn and began practising on the Northern Circuit. Abrahams had
a highly successful run at the British Championship in Chess,
finishing third at Hastings in 1933 and repeating the feat in 1946.
His best finish in the championship came in 1954, when he was
runner-up. He is remembered for his outstanding performance
in the 1946 Anglo-Soviet radio chess match against the Soviet
grandmaster Ragozin. Abrahams won one game and drew two. His
signature move was the Abrahams Defence, a variation of the
Semi-Slav, a move that he and Daniël Noteboom pioneered. In
addition to his many legal works, Abrahams wrote extensively on
chess. His books include *The Chess Mind* (1951) and *Brilliancies in
Chess* (1977). He also wrote about Jewish issues, and published The
Jewish Mind in 1961. He was an active member of the Jewish
community in Liverpool. Abrahams was a Liberal and stood in
the Sheffield Hallam constituency for the 1945 election.

Harold Abrahams

Immortal hero of *Chariots of Fire*
1899–1978

Harold Abrahams was born in Bedford. His father fled Russian-occupied Poland and set up in Bedford as a moneylender and jewellery trader. His mother was a Welsh Jew. Abrahams' older brother, Sydney (Solly), competed in the fourth Olympic games in London and this inspired Harold to take up athletics. He won the public schools' 100 yards and long-jump championships in 1918 and when he went up to Cambridge his talent was spotted. He was selected for the Antwerp Olympics in 1924 and won a gold medal for the 100-yards sprint. His achievement was celebrated in the film *Chariots of Fire* (1981) But the following year Abrahams broke his leg trying to beat the long-jump record and his athletics career was finished. He went on to practise as a barrister, contributed to The Sunday Times as an athletics journalist from 1925 to 1967 and worked as a radio broadcaster for the BBC until 1974. A secular Jew, Abrahams married the D'Oyly Carte singer Sybil Evers and was buried alongside her Church of England grave. He was appointed CBE in 1957. Abrahams was lauded by the Jewish community for his athletic success and in 1923 he was the youngest Jew to be honoured by being invited to a dinner held by the Maccabean Society.

Harold Abrahams crossing the line to win the gold medal in the 100 metres at the 1924 Paris Olympics.

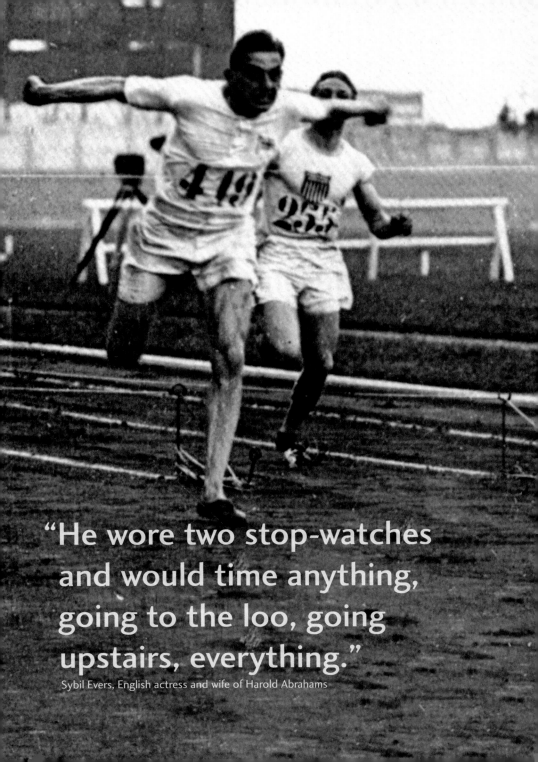

"He wore two stop-watches and would time anything, going to the loo, going upstairs, everything."

Sybil Evers, English actress and wife of Harold Abrahams

Sydney Abrahams
Member of the Colonial
Service and Olympic athlete
1885–1957

Sydney Abrahams was born
in Bedford, England. His father
fled Russian-occupied Poland
and set up in Bedford as a
moneylender and jewellery
trader. Sidney's mother was a
Welsh Jew. In 1906, while still at Cambridge, Abrahams attended
the Intercalated Games in Athens. The event introduced the
first Olympic-style opening ceremony but was not considered
to be part of the formal Olympic cycle and it is referred to as
the "unofficial games". The 1906 games was attended by 900
athletes from 20 countries. Sydney, generally known as Solly, came
fifth in the long jump. In the 1912 Stockholm Olympics he came
11th, then in 1913 he won the Amateur Athletics Association
competition in London. Abrahams went on to study law, joined the
Colonial Service and served as Advocate General in Baghdad as
well as Chief Justice in Uganda and Tanganyika. He was knighted
in 1936 and became Chief Justice of Ceylon (Sri Lanka) that
same year. In 1949 Abrahams returned to Accra, where he had
been Attorney General of the Gold Coast from 1928 to 1933,
and launched a campaign to develop sport that resulted in the
establishment of an Amateur Sports Council. Abrahams was elected
president of Britain's oldest athletics club, the London Athletic
Club, founded in 1863. He was the first Jew to hold this post.

Aaron Alexandre
Wrote important reference
works on chess
1766–1850

Aaron Alexandre was born
in Franconia, Germany. He
trained as a rabbi before
moving to France in 1793.
The French Republic then
employed a policy of religious
toleration, allowing Alexandre to become a citizen of France. Before
focussing on chess, he taught German and made mechanical
inventions. He ultimately dedicated himself to playing, studying
and writing about chess. In 1837 he published his ambitious
work, Encyclopedia of Chess. The book was Alexandre's attempt
to fully catalogue the chess openings, of which there are now
1327 recognised versions. The book established innovations in
chess literature, including new symbols for castling and algebraic
notation. A later work analysed endgames, while *The Beauties of
Chess* (1846) was a collection of 2000 chess problems. These
works became reference material for chess players all over Europe.
Alexandre moved to London in his later years. As a player of the
game, Alexandre's greatest achievement came in 1838 when he
defeated one of the world's greatest players, Howard Staunton, in
London. He was unable to repeat the feat against British chess
master Frederick Deacon the following year, losing 1–0 after Deacon
made the Ponziani Gambit, a variation of the Bishop's Opening.

Mayer Amschel de Rothschild

Banker turned champion
thoroughbred owner
1818–1874

Mayer Amschel de Rothschild
was born in London to Nathan
and Hannah Rothschild. He was
named after his grandfather, who
had established the Rothschild
banking dynasty. His parents were religiously observant. Mayer first
studied at the universities of Leipzig and Heidelberg before moving
to Trinity College, Cambridge. He was the first in the family to receive
an English university education. After this he was apprenticed to
the family business. However, he showed little interest in the work
and was not involved for the rest of his career. His mother Hannah,
believing her children to have weak constitutions, purchased land
in the Buckinghamshire countryside. Here, Mayer established a
stud farm and became a successful race-horse breeder. In 1871 he
won four of the five classic races: the Epsom Derby and Oaks, the
1000 Guineas and the St Leger. In 1847 he was appointed High
Sheriff of Buckinghamshire and then in 1859 he was elected Liberal
MP for Hythe. On his death, his daughter Hannah gave funds
for a lifeboat to be installed at Hythe in his honour. Mayer, and
the wider British Rothschilds, were strong supporters of Jewish
emancipation, advocating political and social freedom for British Jews.

Viktor Barna

Brought table tennis
to the world stage
1911 – 1972

Viktor Barna was born in
Budapest, in the former Austro-
Hungarian empire. Barna, who
was Jewish, was born Gyözö
Braun but decided to change
his name to something that
sounded more Hungarian due to the rising threat of antisemitism
in Hungary. Barna's first experience of table tennis was at a local
sports club in Budapest. By 1929 he was playing for the national
team and helped them to win the 1929 Swaythling Cup. He won
the first of his 22 world titles in Berlin in 1930. Perhaps greater
than his personal achievements in tournaments was his role as
an ambassador for the sport. He combined his love for the game
with his passion for travel and played exhibition games all over
the world to build the profile of the sport. Barna was in America
with his wife Susie when the Second World War broke out but he
relocated to England to fulfil a perceived duty to fight the Nazis. His
military services were ultimately not required, so he entertained
the home front with exhibition games. Barna became a Dunlop
representative after the war and continued to boost the reputation
of table tennis around the world with his trademark trick shots.

Mike Barnard

First-class cricketer in the summer and professional footballer in the winter
1933–2018

Mike Barnard was born in Portsmouth, England. He attended Portsmouth Grammar School. Barnard made his Hampshire debut in 1952 against Glamorgan. He was a right-handed batsman and a medium-pace bowler. Barnard played in 276 first-class matches and nine one-day games for his county. His most successful season with the side was in 1961 when they won the County Championship for the first time in the club's history. Barnard scored 558 runs in 13 matches that season with an average of 29.36. He played 276 first-class matches in his career, scoring 9,314 runs at an average of 22.07. He scored six centuries and 46 half-centuries and made his highest score at Lord's with 128 not out. Barnard took 16 wickets in his career at an average of 35.18 and had best figures of 3/35. Barnard was also a professional footballer. After a spell with Gosport Borough, he made his debut for Portsmouth in December 1953. Barnard appeared for his side in 127 games and scored 26 goals. He left the club in 1959 and joined the non-league club Chelmsford City. Barnard's first school report described him as being "good at games".

Jack "Kid" Berg
He fought his way out of poverty
1909–1991

"The Whitechapel Whirlwind"
was born Judah Bergman in
London's East End. His father
was a tailor and his mother
was an immigrant from Odessa.
The family were Orthodox
and not well-off. Judah would
make a little money by tying a cotton string across the East End
streets that would knock the hats off passing gentlemen's heads.
He would quickly return the hat and would often be given a
shilling for this kind act. He began boxing at the age of 14, going
by the name Jack "Kid" Berg. In 1930 he beat Mushy Callahan
and won the Light Welterweight Championship. However, the
National Boxing Association did not recognise the victory and he
was not officially crowned champion until he beat Goldie Hess a
year later. In 1934 he became the British lightweight champion
by defeating fellow Jewish boxer Harry Mizler. After Berg retired
from boxing in 1945 he worked for the RAF, as a film stuntman
and a restaurant owner. He was proud of his Jewish heritage and
his boxing shorts always displayed a Star of David design.

"Not only could he fight,
but he thought he was
God's gift to the ladies.
You had to watch him
like a hawk."

Ray Arcel

Richard Bergmann
Table tennis player
1919–1970

Richard Bergmann was born in Vienna. He began playing table tennis at the age of 12 and won his first world championship in 1936 at the age of 16. In 1937 he became – and remains – the youngest player ever to win the gold medal in men's singles. A year later he followed up this achievement with a silver. Following the Nazi invasion of Austria, Bergmann fled to England and in 1939 he won his second world singles crown. Together with Victor Barna, he triumphed in the doubles game too, when the pair became world champions. In his adopted country he found incredible success, finishing first in the English singles championships six times and the doubles four times. He earned himself the nickname "Richard the Lionhearted". An ambassador for the sport, he was known for his defensive skills and outstanding footwork. He also made his own rackets; the blade slightly larger than usual, the handle slightly thicker. In the mid-1950s Bergmann became the world's first professional table tennis player, and toured in tandem with the fabled Harlem Globetrotters basketball team. He played in 108 countries and on every continent. He wrote a memoir entitled *21 Up* (1950).

Monty Berman
Goalkeeper and costumier
1912–2002

Morris "Monty" Berman was born in Bethnal Green, London. He was the son and grandson of tailors. As a young man he caught the theatrical bug and joined a Jewish amateur dramatic group called the Plinius Players. His other passion was football, and he played as a reserve goalkeeper for Leyton Orient, also known as the "Os", a team with a strong Jewish tradition. During the Second World War Berman served as a corporal in the RAF, flying with number 5 Bomber Command and the legendary Dam Busters team. He was appointed MBE for his service. After the war he returned to his father's tailoring business and thence to theatrical and film costumes. His firm provided costumes for such classic films as *Lawrence of Arabia*, *Dr Zhivago* and *Star Wars*.

Victor Berliner
Boxing promoter
c.1895–1949

Victor Berliner was born in the East End of London to Polish-born parents. His father was a hairdresser. With his business partner Manny Lyttlestone, Berliner began his career in boxing promotion at the famous Premierland Boxing hall in the 1920s. He became one of the foremost promoters in Britain, managing the Blackfriars Ring, and staging bouts across the UK. He also managed the boxer Harry Mizler from 1933.

Isaac Bitton
Bare-knuckle boxer
1779–1839

Isaac Haim "Abraham" Bitton was born in Amsterdam. His parents were Abraham "Joseph" Bitton and Rachel "David" Bitton. The family were poor street hawkers and, due to the depressed Dutch economy, Bitton and his father emigrated to London, leaving his mother behind. Isaac became a proficient fencer before taking up boxing at the age of 22. In 1801 he rose to fame following a bout against Paddington Tom Jones on London's Wimbledon Common. In 1802 he was paid 20 guineas to fight legendary boxer Maddox, a brutal battle that ended in a draw. Variously known as Isaac The Jew, Isaac Bittoon and "Old Ikey", Bitton was a stout man with a paunch and a punishing punch. His dark curly hair descended into sideburns that twisted into a distinctive J-shaped moustache. He adopted the boxing style of fellow Jew Daniel Mendoza, raising his hands to block punches. He was best known for his 1834 bout with Bill Wood at Willesden Green, which lasted for 36 exhausting rounds and ended in victory for Bitton. He retired from the ring that year but taught fencing and boxing thereafter. Bitton is an ancestor of EastEnders actress June Brown, a fact revealed when Brown featured on BBC1's *Who Do You Think You Are?*

Louis Bookman

Soccer player and cricketer
1890–1943

Louis Bookman was born Louis Buchalter. Along with his father, mother and eight siblings he settled in Dublin. His father, a rabbi, changed the family name in order to better assimilate into society. Young Louis joined a local soccer team in order to make friends, and his aptitude led him to play on the winning side of the under-18s All-Ireland Cup in 1908. Defying his parents, who wanted him to quit the game, Bookman signed for Belfast Celtic in 1910. He went on to be signed by Bradford City, and gained his first Irish cap in 1914 against Wales. In great demand, Bookman signed to West Bromwich Albion for a fee of £875, a fortune in his day. Finding himself a target of vicious antisemitism, Bookman retreated to Ireland for a time, but returned to England with a signing to Luton Town. In 1921 he was selected for a series of internationals. He ended his career in back in his hometown, at Shelbourne in Dublin. Bookman was also an accomplished cricketer, playing for Ireland on 14 occasions. Five years after his death in 1943, the Maccabi Football club was established in Dublin. It is said many of its young Jewish members were inspired by Bookman's achievements.

Victor Buerger
Defeated one of the greatest-
ever chess players
1904–1996

Victor Buerger was born in
Nikolaev, Ukraine. He was
a member of the London
Chess Club. He had a strong
tournament career, consistently
finishing in a good ranking at a
time when one of the greatest-ever players of the game, Alexander
Alekhine, was dominating many of the competitions. He played at
Pardubice in 1923 and tied for fifth–seventh place, before tying for
seventh–ninth place the following year. Buerger tied for first place
with British chess master Frederick Yates at the 1926 tournament
in London. He continued this strong run of form the following
year, tying for third–fourth place in Hastings before winning at
Cheltenham in 1928. More success followed in 1929 when Buerger
tied for second–third in London, and then for first–third the
next year. Buerger could only take 11th place at London in 1932
as again he saw Alekhine win a major tournament. But in 1937
Buerger scored his greatest achievement in the game, defeating
Alekhine at Margate. Subsequent journalism drew attention to
the shoddy playmaking in the game due to intense time pressure.
When Alekhine squandered a winning position halfway through
the game the Chess Journal called the blunder "probably the most
incredible double oversight in the history of first-class chess".

Tony Bullimore
Survived five days in the
Southern Ocean with only
a bar of chocolate
1939–2018

Tony Bullimore was born in
Bristol. He was a Jewish sailor
best known for his participation
in the treacherous 1996–7
Vendée Globe, a solo non-
stop round-the-world yacht race. The fleet tackled heavy weather
throughout the race but conditions worsened in the Southern
Ocean, where several of the sailors capsized. Canadian sailor Gerry
Roufs disappeared and was never found. Bullimore, who was sailing
the Exide Challenger, had contended with winds of up to 80 knots
for almost a day when the keel of his yacht snapped. He capsized
near 52°S 100°E, around 1,500 miles from Australia, and was
assumed lost by most of the media. Bullimore survived in an air
pocket in the upside-down boat, keeping his spirits up by singing
sea shanties and praying. He had only a chocolate bar to sustain
him for five days. Bullimore was saved by the HMAS Adelaide
after they discovered his upturned yacht and knocked on the hull.
Despite his ordeal, Bullimore did not lose his passion for sailing
and attempted to break the solo round-the-world record in 2007.

Jack Solomons was for many years Britain's premier boxing promoter.

IN 1950, 1,800 boxers
by the British Box
Control. In the same y
800 promotions. Last y
only 420 boxers and a
motions. Boxing in the
small halls had virtuall
ing the period, and aud
ed a taste for only th
in the biggest promoti
supply and demand
the cost of a good
rapidly, and only a fe
afford to pay it.
    This inflation be
Harry Levene—who
the twenties as the
leader George Lans
—and the 42-year-o
a director of the T
cates, which run a
shops, property co
essential compone
fight, Viewsport.

Sam Burns, one of the top managers

Sam Burns

Boxing promoter
1914–1994

Sam Burns was born in Cannon Street on the edge of the City of London. At the age of 14 he left school to work in the tape-room of the London Evening News. Three years later he joined Sporting Life, where he wrote about horseracing under the pseudonym "Bendigo". His true love, however, was boxing and under the pseudonym "Straight Left" he wrote about his passion. After the Second World War he joined promoter and fellow Jew Jack Solomons as a general manager. The partnership lasted for ten years. Burns managed many outstanding British fighters, including featherweight Bobby Neil, middleweight Tony Sibson and welterweight Eddie Thomas. He managed the Finnegan brothers, Olympic gold medallists Chris and Kevin. He also managed World Middleweight Champion Terry Downes, with whom he went on to establish a betting shop business. Their association grew to 90 shops, and was eventually taken over by Hills. Burns himself was managing director of William Hill from 1972 to 1981. He was a premier figure in the British boxing scene for more than half a century, and was also heavily involved in horseracing.

Sid Burns
Boxer
1890–1948

Sid Burns was born in 1890 in Aldgate, London. He became a significant figure in British boxing around the time of the First World War. He fought opponent Johnny Summers twice in title matches, once for the English Welterweight Championship and once for Welterweight Championship of the British Empire in Australia. In both bouts he lost on points. Burns also travelled to America, fighting the American Mike Gibbons in Madison Square Garden. Burns was operating at the very top of his sport, taking on opponents such as Summers, Sid Stagg, Tommy Gibbons and the legendary George Carpentier. He formed an intense rivalry with his former sparring partner Ted "Kid" Lewis. Burns retired in 1920.

Horatio Caro
Chess master
1862–1920

Horatio Caro was born in Newcastle upon Tyne. He spent most of his chess-playing career in Berlin. He played several matches of note. 1892 was a year of mixed fortunes, which saw him drawing with Curt von Bardeleben, but losing to Szymon Winawer. In 1897 he was defeated by fellow Jewish master Jacques Mieses. In 1903 he drew once again with Bardeleben, and in 1905 he won against Moritz Lewitt. Caro achieved notable success at tournament level. In 1904 he won the Berlin Championship half a point ahead of Ossip Bernstein and Rudolf Spielmann. He also either won or was placed at Vienna, Nuremberg, Coberg and Barmen. His greatest claim to fame is the Caro–Kann defence to which he gave his name. He developed this play alongside Marcus Kann, and analysed it in his own periodical Bruederschaft in 1886. The Caro–Kahn defence is classified as a "Semi Open Game" against the King's Pawn Opening, which often leads to good endgames for black. Caro used his own defence to beat Mieses in 17 moves.

Benny Casofsky
Table tennis player
1919–1987

Benny Casofsky was of Jewish descent. Along with Leslie Cohen and Hyman Lurie he formed the Manchester team that won the Wilmott Cup (National Team Championship) on three occasions. Even in such strong company he was ranked Manchester number one. He rose to become the president of the Manchester and District League. Casofsky also found success at an international level. He was part of the fabled 1947 World Table Tennis Championships in the Swaythling Cup – the men's team event – with Eric Filby, Ernest Bubley, Johnny Leach and fellow Jew George "Eli" Goodman.

Ernest Cassel

Merchant banker and
racehorse owner
1852 – 1921

Ernst Cassel was born in
Cologne, Germany, the son of
Jacob Cassel, a banker. After
working in a bank in Cologne
he came to Liverpool, without
means, in 1869, and found work
with a firm of German grain merchants. He was then employed by
Henri Louis Bischoffscheim, a major merchant banker in London,
and was also a close friend of the multimillionaire Maurice, Baron de
Hirsch. From 1884 until 1910 Cassel was an independent merchant
banker in London, building a vast web of international finance that
included investments in Latin America, South Africa and the United
States. Along with de Hirsch, Cassel was one of the closest friends
of Edward, Prince of Wales. Jealous tongues scoffed at the "Windsor
Cassels", while Lady Paget complained that the prince was "always
surrounded by a bevy of Jews and a ring of racing people". Cassel
spent a large portion of his considerable fortune on his stables at
Newmarket but his horses found little success on the racecourse.
Despite his royal patronage Cassel faced the difficulties shared
by other wealthy Jews wishing to assimilate into British society. It
is thought that his later conversion to Catholicism, following the
example of his wife Annette Maxwell, was an attempt to gain wider
acceptance among the ruling elite.

Hartwig Cassel
Chess journalist and editor
1850–1929

Hartwig Cassel was born at Konitz, in former West Prussia. His father, Dr Aaron Cassel, was a rabbi. Hartwig received his education at the Real-Gymnasium in Landsberg-an-der-Warthe. He emigrated to England in 1879, where he began his career in journalism in Bradford, as chess editor on the Observer-Budget. He went on to write chess articles for both metropolitan and provincial papers and periodicals. In addition to his blossoming journalistic career Cassel began to take on an organisational role in the world of chess. He established the Yorkshire County Chess Club and arranged the Blackburne–Gunsberg match at Bradford in 1887. The following year he arranged the International Chess Masters' Tournament in the same city. In 1889 Cassel left England for Havana, where he joined an English-American newspaper syndicate to report the Tchigorin–Gunsberg match. 1890 found him in New York, where he became chess editor of the papers the Sun and the Staats-Zeitung. There too Cassel was an important figure behind the scenes in the US chess world, establishing the Staats-Zeitung and Rice trophies and arranging the first cable chess match between Manhattan and British chess clubs. Cassel also invented a chess cable code.

Aubrey Cohen
Footballer

Aubrey Cohen was a very successful Jewish Sunday League player who had a connection to Man United in his youth and young adulthood. He was selected for the Manchester United squad in the late 1940s, the era of the fabled "Busby Babes". Although he didn't make it as a regular in the first team, he was very close to that team and their manager Matt Busby. Cohen was traumatised by the Munich air crash because he lost a lot of his friends. Yet his relationship with Busby extended beyond his time at the club. Letters survive from their handwritten correspondence, including an RSVP note to a wedding invitation, which Matt Busby sent to him, and an invitation to training at Manchester United. "Bring your own shorts, stockings and towel. And boots," it says, evoking an era so distant from today.

Avi Cohen

Footballer

1956–2010

Avraham Cohen was born in Cairo. He played for the Israeli club Maccabi Tel Aviv, where his skills attracted the attention of Liverpool manager Bob Paisley. Cohen joined Liverpool in the summer of 1979 for a fee of £200,000. He was the first Israeli footballer to play for an English club in the top division. He quickly integrated, and his good humour and determination to learn good English endeared him to his teammates. 1980 was Cohen's year. He scored one of Liverpool's decisive goals in the 4–1 defeat of Aston Villa in the League Cup. He then went from hero to villain in the eyes of the Israeli press when, later that year, he decided to play for Liverpool against Southampton on Yom Kippur. The commentary may have affected his game as he gave away a goal with a weak pass. In 1981 Cohen returned to Maccabi Tel Aviv. He spent one more season in Britain, for Glasgow Rangers, from 1987–8. He made 64 international appearances for his native Israel, captaining the team 33 times. He became manager of the Israeli Maccabi Herzliya, a team for which he had played, and subsequently managed other Israeli clubs. Cohen also served as head of the Israeli Football Players' Association.

The story of the Tony Cohen Cup

Tony Cohen
Footballer
1935–1966

Y ROB CLYNE

• **FOOTBALL** May 5, 2013 will be the 5th anniversary of the first Tony Cohen Memorial Trophy final - the conclusion MJSL's second oldest tournament is a highlight of the football calendar.

Tony Cohen passed away after a battle with Hodgkin's lymphoma, then Hodgkin's Disease, on October 20, 1966. He was years old. Popular and well liked for his sy-going personality, his death came as great shock to the community.

MJSL Honorary Life Vice President ny Sheldon remembers him fondly. He always had a smile on his face, he dn't have a bad bone in his body. I n't even remember him committing foul."

Indeed, Cohen was highly regarded his football ability. He was a classy side forward who thrived in the old mber 10 position. "I used to think 'Oh ar, he's playing!' He was a cracking

approached Sheldon, then MJSL chairman, a year after his untimely passing He said: "The family decided to do something to commemorate Tony's life."

Waterpark's close connection w Cohen created an overwhelming des ral tournament in 1968. Excitingly, t final would be contested between Nor

Manchester a Tony Cohen own Waterpa 2nd team.

There follow a difficult tea selection pro ess. The manag ment attempt to fill the tea with 1st tea players, causing real stir among

Tony Cohen in his playing days

the 2nd team.

After negotiating a U-turn on this de

Tony Cohen was an inside forward who played in the number 10 position. He was highly regarded for his footballing ability. He played for Waterpark, based in Broughton Park, which was the north's biggest social club in the 1960s. Thanks in large part to Cohen, Waterpark was the top team of the day, winning trophy after trophy. Tony Sheldon remembers Cohen as a "cracking player with great ball skills." Sadly the popular and well-liked player died of Hodgkin's lymphoma in 1966, at the age of 31. His family decided to do something to commemorate Cohen's life, and founded a tournament in his name. The inaugural tournament took place in 1968 between North Manchester and Cohen's own Waterpark second team. The latter secured an emotional 3–1 win for their lost teammate. The winners' medals were awarded by Cohen's brother Leslie and his nephew Howard. The Tony Cohen Cup has now been awarded for over 45 years.

Manny Cussins
Football chairman
1905–1987

Manny Cussins made his fortune in the furniture retail business. He began by selling furniture from a handcart in his native Hull at the age of 13. He rose to be chairman of Waring & Gillow, the company famed for fitting out high-end yachts and liners, including the Lusitania and the Queen Mary. In 1961 Cussins joined the board of directors at Leeds United F.C. He served as the club's chairman from 1972 to 1983. Cussins saw several managers come and go at Leeds. In his era the legendary Don Revie was replaced by Brian Clough. Under Clough, the team performed poorly, and after just 44 days Cussins famously sacked him. Cussins was expansion-minded and expressed an intention to take Leeds to victory in the European Cup. This almost happened; Clough was replaced by Jimmie Armfield, who took the club to the 1975 final of the cup, but Leeds lost to Bayern Munich. Impatient for success, Cussins dismissed Armfield in 1978. Jock Stein came next, also lasting just 44 days. Jimmy Adamson and Allan Clarke were unable to stop the decline, and Cussins' tenure as chairman ended in the club's relegation in 1982. A well-known workaholic, Cussins was fond of saying, "Retirement turns men into cabbages."

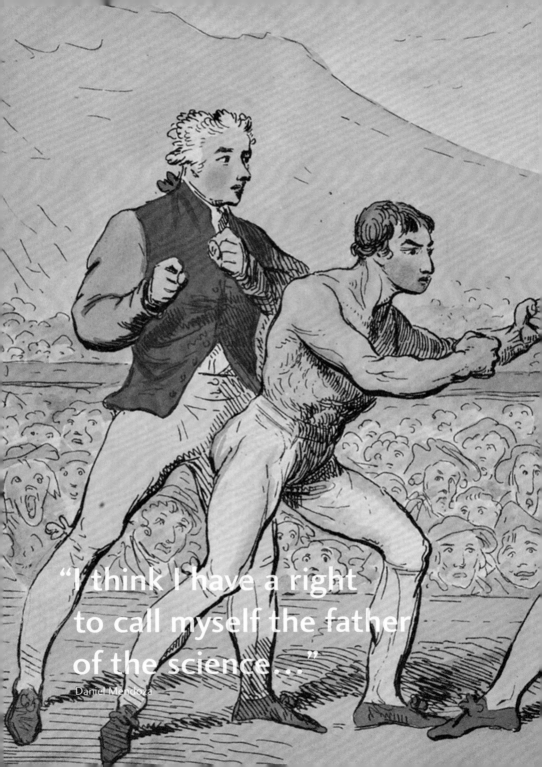

"I think I have a right
to call myself the father
of the science..."
Daniel Mendoza

Daniel Mendoza

Daniel Mendoza was Heavyweight Champion of England from 1792–95, and the first middleweight to ever win the Heavyweight Championship of the World. His book *The Art of Boxing* was a modern "scientific" approach to the sport and an approach that every subsequent boxer has learned from.

MENDOZA.

Daniel Mendoza, champion of England 1792–95, was of Portuguese-Jewish descent.

Daniel Mendoza

Wynn Wheldon

Author of "The Fighting Jew – The Life
and Times of Daniel Mendoza"

Following a bout of ill-health, possibly malaria, Daniel Mendoza, recently recognised as England's champion boxer after his demolition of William Ward, left the foetid air of London for a few days' recuperation at Windsor. Walking one evening in the Great Park, he was summoned, 'in a very abrupt manner' (rarely a clever manner where the easily-insulted Mendoza was concerned) to attend a group of distinguished looking gentlemen on a nearby terrace. He acceded to the request, and spent a while talking at some length with the most senior member of the party, who seemed to know a good deal about boxing. Eventually, a young woman approached them, with a small boy in tow. She asked Mendoza if it would be in order for the small boy to throw a punch at him, so that he might 'boast at a subsequent opportunity of having at an earlier period of his life, struck a professed pugilist on Windsor terrace.' The knowledgeable old man was King George III and the young woman his daughter, Charlotte, the Princess Royal. Who the boy was - well, George's male grandchildren could have fathered a small island republic.

Daniel Mendoza was as comfortable talking with royals as he was fighting off muggers (he was once attacked on the Strand: 'I found ye sharp and left you flat' he apparently remarked after putting his assailants to the ground). Pierce Egan, great recorder of the prize ring and life in London at the time, described Mendoza as 'intelligent and communicative', and so he was. Not only did he write one of the first instruction manuals describing the 'science' of the sport, *The Art of Boxing* (1789), he is also responsible for the first autobiography by a professional sportsman, *Memoirs of the Life of Daniel Mendoza* ('New Edition', 1816), a book that remains a thoroughly enjoyable read, full of anecdote, pride and self-deprecation. More than all this, he is credited with raising the social status of Jews and making the streets of London safe for them to walk on without fear of attack.

There had been Jewish boxers before Daniel Mendoza, but none achieved anything remotely like his success, or had his *elan* both as a fighter and a teacher. He liked to sign himself 'P.P.' - professor of pugilism – in gentle mockery perhaps of more academic honours, but also to suggest quite seriously that pugilism could be taught. Mendoza was small for a boxer, five foot seven and around eleven stone (150 pounds, 70 kg), and those he fought were invariably bigger and stronger. Mendoza developed a defensive strategy that depended on lightning quickness of response for its offensive power. The sluggers who had dominated boxing found themselves out-thought and out-manoeuvred.

His first great public fight, in the presence of the Prince of Wales, was at Barnet racecourse, where he defeated Sam Martin, the Bath butcher. It must rank high in the great days of British Jewish history. Mendoza was brought back to Duke's Place, Aldgate, the very heart of Jewish life in London, in triumph and jubilation, with song and celebration. The fight that followed, with Richard Humphries, the 'gentleman boxer', made him a star beyond the East End of London, for although he lost, the result had been controversial. 'The little black bruiser' had gained a moral victory in proving himself the equal to one of the best that Anglican England could set against him. The two men fought again and again, making a trilogy that came to be regarded as the *ne plus ultra* of 'scientific' boxing. Mendoza was the victor in both the succeeding bouts.

The eighteenth century French writer Nicholas Chamfort defined the state of celebrity as 'being known by those who do not know you', and Daniel Mendoza was undoubtedly that. There were prints and portraits and mugs and jugs and medals, all the familiar paraphernalia that surrounds renown. Several such items are on view in the Jewish Museum. It is arguable that Mendoza was the first sporting superstar of the modern age. It is remarkable that he should have been Jewish.

He was born in Aldgate in either 1764 or 1765, depending on whether we believe his own questionable memory, or the records of Bevis Marks synagogue. His great great grandfather, David, had made his way from Seville to London by way of Amsterdam. Abraham and Esther, Daniel's parents, were 'in the middling class of society', and able at least to afford some schooling for their children. Dan was proud of the Hebrew he had learned, but was put out to work at 13, apprentice to a glass cutter. It was the first of a series of jobs he lost due to his inability to let insult pass without vigorous physical punishment. His came to be known as a defender of Jewish honour (though his first professional fight was on the Sabbath) and as an exceptional street fighter. He came to the attention of another young fighter, someone who had begun to teach, by the name of Richard Humphries. Humphries seconded Mendoza through his early bouts, but the two fell out, it is not entirely clear why, and the enmity of past friends added a kind of spice to the battles between them that were to come.

There are suggestions that in 1782, at the age of seventeen, Daniel Mendoza robbed a man in Aldgate Street, was caught, made his escape by stabbing his captor in the hand, made off, was re-

Mendoza v Humphreys, Staffordshire pottery jug c.1800 and depicting a famous fight between Mendoza and Richard Humphreys in 1788.

Mendoza v Humphreys, illustration of the aftermath of the fight in 1788.

arrested, tried, and transported to the coast of west Africa. Someone called either Daniel Mendoza or Daniel Mondoca (according to the Old Bailey transcript) was certainly tried for the crime. As far as can be ascertained the only other Daniel Mendoza living in London at the time was Dan's uncle (also his father-in-law-to-be), who was in his forties. If the culprit was Dan Mendoza, the boxer, it seems strange that this was never used against him. The judge had wanted him executed. That Daniel Mendoza was a violent man can hardly be denied, though in his memoirs he regrets not having made a life as a confectioner. In 1795, he was found guilty of assaulting two washerwomen who had asked to be paid. There was a suggestion that they had insulted his wife, but the attack was brutal, and one of the women, Rachel Joel, 'could not sit with any ease for months afterwards'.

Daniel Mendoza became 'champion', an honour from which no emolument arose, other than the acclaim of the Fancy, when he beat William Ward (or Warr) at Smitham Bottom, near Croydon, to the south of London, in 1792. The title had been vacant since the retirement of Big Ben Brian (or Brain) after his victory over Tom Johnson. Brian had so damaged himself in that bout that he was unable to fight again, and indeed died of his wounds. Mendoza beat Ward again in 1794. No-one now questioned his supremacy, and so, the following year, at Hornchurch in Essex, he was favourite to beat an inexperienced fighter called John Jackson. The latter was a much bigger man – he was six foot tall and weighed around fifteen stone - and a natural athlete, but he had spent very little time in the prize ring. But it was heavyweight versus middleweight. Mendoza, nonetheless, seemed to be at the very least holding his own until Jackson grabbed at the hair that Mendoza liked to wear long and holding him so began to pummel his head with blow after blow. Thus did Daniel Mendoza lose his championship to another 'gentleman', and thus did boxing gain as its 'commander-in-chief' a man his pupil, the poet Byron, described as having 'the best physique in Europe'.

Some commentators thought that Mendoza might have thrown the fight, but he was far too proud a man to have done that, however dire his financial straits might have been. For Daniel Mendoza's uselessness with money is one of the most pitiable aspects of his life. He made a a great deal of money from his fight with Sam Martin alone – a thousand pounds, it has been estimated – and might easily have set himself for life by the time he beat Humphries in their third fight, at Doncaster. He made money too from teaching at his own academy at Capel Court in the City and at the Lyceum in the Strand. He taught privately, too. And when not doing this he was touring the country, exhibiting, sparring. He visited almost every major city in the British Isles, from Liskeard to Dumfries, from Dublin to Norwich; he wrote books; he even lectured at Oxford, and yet he was relentlessly pursued ('harassed' was Mendoza's own word) by creditors from 1795 onwards, and was not infrequently in prison for debt. Having said which, almost everyone in the age spent some time in prison for debt, from Oliver Goldsmith to Emma Hamilton. The mystery remains as to how Mendoza managed to spend quite so much money.

His own vague explanation, that he had 'almost unavoidably adopted an expensive mode of living, and having, from the nature of my profession, formed connections with persons of larger incomes than myself, the consequence was, I had frequently been led into costly and extravagant pursuits', rather suggests gambling, which the historian M. Dorothy George maintained was 'interwoven with the fabric of society to an astonishing extent'. Georgian bucks and rakes would bet on anything, and usually vast sums of money. Mendoza tried to wean himself off boxing, taking work as a recruiting officer, as a Sheriff's officer, opening a shop selling oil, a shop selling snuff, and was given the funds to take over a pub, *The Children in the Wood* (which he renamed the *Admiral Nelson*) in the Whitechapel Road. None of these adventures came to anything. In 1806 he fought an old friend, Henry Lee, probably for money. He won, easily. In 1809 he lent himself and his followers to John Kemble, who was attempting to enforce new prices on spectators after the rebuilding of the Theatre Royal, Covent Garden. Their intervention was extremely unpopular. In 1820 Mendoza fought his last battle, against Tom Owen, five years Mendoza's junior, but still fifty years old. Mendoza lost in five minutes.

Despite numerous 'benefits' held on boxing days at such venues as the Fives Court, Royal Tennis Court (both in the West End) and the Minerva Rooms (in the City), Daniel Mendoza's decline into destitution appears to be inevitable. State aid to the poor was limited to Anglicans, and the Jewish charities were stretched by the accelerating influx of poor Jews from eastern Europe. His children, of whom he and Esther (whom he had married in 1788) had as many as eleven, did not flourish: three were transported for various crimes, one probably spent time in one of the prison hulks on the Thames, others disappeared into obscurity. Their last born, Matilda, managed to emigrate to Australia voluntarily.

Daniel Mendoza died at one thirty in the morning on September 3rd, 1836, in Horsehoe Alley, Petticoat Lane. His death followed 'a long and lingering illness, embittered by poverty and a succession of vicissitudes'. He was buried the following day at the Nuevo Cemetery for Spanish and Portugese Jews at Mile End. In 1855 seven thousand graves were moved to Brentwood, in Essex. Mendoza's is unmarked. What became of Esther has gone unrecorded.

For the time being, the glory passed to Mendoza's successors – Jackson, Jem Belcher, Tom Cribb, Tom Spring, the 'non-pareil' Jack Randall – but they are not now the names to conjure with. That honour belongs to those like the black boxers Bill Richmond and Tom Molineaux, and Dan Mendoza, men who did more than simply knock the living daylights out of their antagonists. These were characters who changed the world in which they lived. They may not have intended to do so, but this takes nothing away from their achievements. Daniel Mendoza, a man intemperate, violent, charismatic, mischievous, and, finally and forever, heroic, was a Londoner, a proud Englishman, and, emphatically, 'one-two', a Jew.

Opposite Daniel Mendoza, illustrated print from 1790 showing Mendoza's third fight with Richard Humphreys. The fight lasted for about an hour and five minutes and was decided in favour of Mendoza.

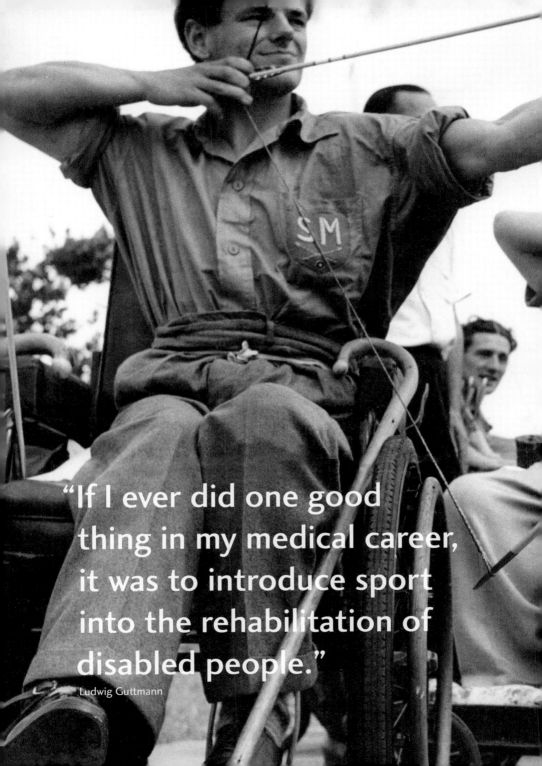

"If I ever did one good thing in my medical career, it was to introduce sport into the rehabilitation of disabled people."

Ludwig Guttmann

Biographies D – H

On the same day that King George VI opened the 1948 Olympic Games in London, Dr Ludwig Guttman presided over a wheel chair archery competition in the grounds of Stoke Mandeville Hospital. This tournament was the first step towards the Paralympic Games.

Jacques Davidson
Chess master
1890–1969

Jacques Davidson was born in Amsterdam. He lived in London for a number of years prior to the First World War. He learned chess by playing against his father for a stake. The winnings were never paid over but the thought occurred that he could play wealthy Englishmen for money. He turned to another native of the Netherlands for advice – Rudolf Loman, the Dutch chess master, became his mentor. In 1911 Davidson won a match against Edward Sergeant in London. Davidson went on to be placed numerous times at Tunbridge Wells, Cologne, The Hague, Berlin, Spa and Utrecht. During the 1920s Davidson won two victories in his native Amsterdam, but in the 1930s lost there three times.

Bernard Delfont
Director of Leyton Orient FC
1909–1994

Bernard Delfont was born
Boruch Winogradsky in Tokmak,
Russia. He was the son of Isaac
Winogradsky (1879–1915), who
worked in a clothing factory. The
family, which included Bernard's
brothers Leslie and Lew Grade,
migrated to London in 1911. Bernard took the name "Delfont" in
1929 to distinguish himself from his brother Lew. Both had become
professional dancers and actors. From 1937 Bernard Delfont was
a major theatrical impresario and presented over 200 shows in
London and New York, including 21 Royal Variety Performances
between 1958 and 1978. Delfont became chief executive of EMI Ltd.,
a company that owned 300 cinemas and four West End theatres.
From 1961-1968 he was director of Leyton Orient Football Club.
He once memorably advised theatrical impresario Andrew Lloyd-
Webber: "Let me tell you something, my boy. Never waste your
money on a football club." But under Delfont the team flourished,
becoming known as the showbiz club, as Delfont brought his
celebrity friends to see the team. Before one FA cup-tie, Delfont
brought comedian Arthur Askey to entertain the terraces. Askey used
his trademark prop, a long whip, to exercise a little crowd control,
urging supporters to huddle together more tightly on the terraces.
Delfont was knighted in 1974 and awarded a life peerage in 1976.

Mickey Duff
Boxing promoter
1929–2014

Mickey Duff was born Monek Prager into a Hassidic Jewish family in Tarnow, Poland. In 1937, upon the rise of Hitler in neighbouring Germany, his rabbi father fled to Britain, followed by his wife and children. The family settled in the East End of London, where young Monek formed a passion for boxing. In the face of his parents' disapproval, but inspired by boxing hero Jack "Kid" Berg, he began training in boxing gyms and adopted the ring name Mickey Duff. The name came from a character played by Jimmy Cagney. "I hit and I ran" was how Duff described his fighting style. Despite his great success in the ring – winning 61 out of 69 bouts – Duff believed he would never reach the top and turned to management. He went on to have a direct influence on the successes of 19 world champions, including Terry Downes, Henry Cooper and Lloyd Honeyghan. With his business partners Harry Levene, Jarvis Astaire, Mike Barrett and Terry Lawless, Duff put on sell out shows such as Muhammad Ali v Henry Cooper at Highbury Football ground in 1966. From the 1970s onwards Duff, an inveterate gambler, was paid by Caesar's Palace in Las Vegas to act as their boxing consultant.

"If you want loyalty,
buy a dog."
Mickey Duff

Samuel "Dutch Sam" Elias

Boxer

1775 – 1816

"Dutch Sam" was born Samuel Elias in London. His parents were émigrés from Holland and he grew up in Whitechapel. He attended Daniel Mendoza's boxing academy, and made his debut in the ring in 1801. Small in stature at only 5'6", and weighing only 130 lbs, Elias had no trouble defeating larger men. A case in point was his rout of the celebrated Caleb Baldwin in 1804, a champion who weighed in at nearly 200 lbs. His ferocity earned him the second nickname "The Terrible Jew". His regular rival was Tom Belcher, whom he fought three times. The 1806 bout ended in a round-57 knock out for Sam. The second match, the following year, was a draw. The third was a 36-round stoppage for Sam. In all three bouts Daniel Mendoza acted as Sam's second, and was in his corner. Dutch Sam retired undefeated after 100 contests, a remarkable feat. He was prompted to make a comeback after antisemitic goading from fellow boxer William Nosworthy. After an epic battle Nosworthy knocked out Dutch Sam in the 50th round. Dutch Sam proudly trained on three glasses of gin a day, and frequently entered the ring drunk.

Maurice Fox
Chess master
1898–1988

Maurice Fox was born in the former Russian Empire. At the end of 1898, the family emigrated to London, where Fox was educated at the University of London. Upon graduation in 1921, Fox moved once again, this time to Canada in 1923. During his first year in Canada, Fox entered the Canadian Chess Championship in Hamilton and took second behind much more established Canadian chess champion John Morrison. In the years that followed, Fox had numerous successes on the chess circuit in Canada. He was Canadian champion in 1927, 1929, 1931 following a play-off, 1932, 1935, 1938, 1940 and 1949. Fox also made a name for himself on the international chess scene, playing in several United States Opens. In the 1956 Canadian Open Chess Championship at Montreal, at the age of 58, Fox beat 13-year-old prodigy Bobby Fischer, a future World Champion.

Selim Franklin
Pioneer and chess master
1814–1885

Selim Franklin was born in Liverpool. His parents were Miriam and Lewis Franklin, a banker and importer of marble. He became a world-ranked chess player at London's chess clubs such as the Westminster Chess Club and Simpson's Divan Chess Room. Following the discovery of gold in California, in 1849 Franklin boarded the *St George* to San Francisco, where he ran a successful business as an estate agent and auctioneer. In 1857 he returned to his first love of chess, featuring on the Planning & Rules committee for the first American Chess Congress, held in New York. He established San Francisco as a centre of world chess, founding the California Chess Congress in 1858. Franklin won the tournament himself, winning the prize of "a costly gold watch". In the same year, following the gold trail once more, he relocated to Victoria, there to be engaged by the government. He was only the third Jew to be elected to the legislature in British North America. Franklin returned to London to participate in several high-profile chess matches between 1868 and 1871. His final match was against fellow Jewish chess master Johannes Zukertort in 1884. Following his death the Franklin River on the Alberni Canal was named after him.

Leslie Goldberg
Footballing right back
1918–1985

Leslie Goldberg was born in Leeds, the son of an immigrant boot riveter. He was educated at Lovell Road School and the Leeds Jewish Institute. Both foundations supported physical education in an attempt to counter the "Jewish weakling" stereotypes perpetuated by antisemites. Goldberg's beloved sports master Nat Collins encouraged his pupils to, literally and metaphorically, "fight back". Goldberg made his first appearance for Leeds United in 1937. His trajectory was interrupted by the Second World War, when he saw active service in India, and in peacetime he resumed his playing career at Reading. There, due to the relatively small Jewish community, he felt painfully exposed, and began to experience antisemitism. He changed his name to Les Gaunt a year later, but the camouflage did not work. His career ended in 1950 when he broke his leg badly in a vicious tackle during a match against Norwich. It was thought that the tackle was racially motivated. Goldberg is remembered as the first Jew to play for Leeds United, to appear on a cigarette card and to be mentioned on a Pathé newsreel.

Albert Goodman
Footballer
1890–1959

Albert Goodman was born in Dalston, London. He began his footballing career as captain of the London Fields School eleven. He then played for non-league teams London Fields, Tufnell Park, Tottenham Thursday, Maidstone United and Croydon Common. In 1919 he hit the big time when he signed for Tottenham Hotspur, and in 1920 won a Football League Division 2 Championship medal with the club. In the course of his career at Tottenham he played 17 matches and scored one goal in all competitions. He went on to play for Margate, then in 1921 signed to Charlton Athletic. There he played in seven different positions, played 136 matches and scored 15 goals. Goodman made appearances at Gillingham and Clapton Orient and ended his career at Guildford City. Following his retirement he coached Tooting Town. Albert Goodman was known as "a glutton for work, full of dash". During the course of his career he was given the nickname "Kosher" and in the 1920s he appeared on four different cigarette cards, an undoubted accolade for a footballer of those times.

Harry Golombek

First person awarded an
OBE for services to chess
1911 – 1995

Harry Golombek was born in
the East End of London. His
family had migrated from Poland.
Golombek attended Wilson's
Grammar School and helped the
school achieve unprecedented
success in the London Schools' Team Championship. He won the
London Boys' Championship in 1929. In 1935 Golombek made
the first of his six appearances at the Chess Olympics. He studied
at London University before joining the codebreakers at Bletchley
Park. His chess career flourished after the war, and he won the
first of three British Championships in 1947. He also had great
success on the international stage, finishing first in tournaments
in Leeuarden and Berne. Golombek's deep understanding of
the game earned him an appointment as chess correspondent
at *The Times*, followed in 1955 by a column in the *Observer*. He
went on to write more than 30 books on the subject, including
his essential beginners' guide, *The Game of Chess* (1954). In
1966 Golombek became the first person to be awarded an OBE
for services to chess. While at Bletchley Park, Golombek would
defeat Alan Turing at chess even after giving him a queen start.

George Goodman
Table tennis player

George "Eli" Goodman was an international table tennis player. He represented Manchester at a national level and was first capped against Wales in 1946. He was part of the fabled England team that competed at the 1947 World Table Tennis Championships in the Swaythling Cup. The Swaythling Cup was a men's team event, and the cup itself donated in 1926 by Lady Baroness Swaythling, mother of Jewish player Ivor Montagu. Goodman's teammates were Ernest Bubley, Eric Filby, Johnny Leach and fellow Jew Benny Casofsky.

Leslie Grade

Talent agent and
football manager
1916–1979

Leslie Grade was born Laszlo (or
Lazarus) Winogradsky, in London.
His parents, Isaac and Olga,
worked in the textile industry.
His family had emigrated from
Tokmak, Ukraine, during the
pogroms. Leslie was raised in Stepney alongside siblings Lew and
Bernard. He left school at 14 to establish a career in showbusiness,
and alongside his brother Lew became a respected talent agent. In
the 1940s he had such star talent as Danny Kaye and Bob Hope
on his books. With his friend and fellow Jew Harry Zussman, Grade
served, for many years, as director of Leyton Orient F.C. He presided
over the club in the glory days of the 60s and 70s when Orient
were promoted to the First Division of English Football for the
only time in their history. Due to the three Grade brothers on the
board, numerous stars of the day visited the club, including Cliff
Richard, Shirley Bassey and Pat Boone. However, alone among the
three brothers, Leslie was not awarded a peerage or a knighthood.

Lew Grade

Impresario and
television executive
1906 - 1998

Born Louis Winogradsky in
Tokmak, Russia, the brother of
Sir Bernard Delfont and Leslie
Grade, Lew Grade came to
England with his family in 1911.
Like his brother Bernard he was
a professional dancer and then a theatrical impresario. He is best
known as one of the formative figures in independent television. At
his peak in the 1970s he headed a great empire of the entertainment
industry. The corpulent, cigar-chomping, wisecracking Grade was
one of the few British impresarios who resembled the Hollywood
moguls of legend. Grade was responsible for such television shows
as *The Saint*, *The Muppet Show* and *Thunderbirds*, and for classic films
including *On Golden Pond* (1981) Alongside his brothers Bernard
Delfont and Leslie Grade, Lew served on the board of Leyton Orient
Football Club, a team with a strong Jewish tradition. The Grade
brothers brought a sprinkling of showbiz to the club, and brought
along the stars from their agency's stable to support the 'Os', as the
team were known. One special guest, the American pop singer Pat
Boone, sent each player a special straw hat as a memento of his visit.

Isidor Gunsberg

Operator of the Mephisto
chess automaton
1854–1930

Isidor Gunsberg was born in
Budapest, Hungary. He moved
to Great Britain in 1876 and
became a British citizen in
1908. Gunsberg's chess career
began as the operator for the
chess automaton Mephisto. Mephisto was a remote-controlled
chess-playing devil that won the Counties Chess Association in
London in 1878. Gunsberg went on tour with the machine in 1879.
Free from the devilish guise, Gunsberg became one of the greatest
players of the game in the world. 1885 saw him win a national
tournament in London as well as the fourth German Chess Congress
in Hamburg. The following year he scored victories against fellow
greats of the game, Joseph Blackburne and Henry Bird. He tied
for first with Amos Burn in the 1887 London tournament before
drawing with Russian Romantic chess player and future world
championship challenger, Mikhail Chigorin, in 1890. Gunsberg
came desperately close to winning the World Chess Championship
in 1891, ultimately losing to William Steinitz in a tight game with
four wins, six losses and nine draws. Gunsberg was rated 2560
on the Elo rating , the system used to compare relative skill
levels in chess. In 1916 he successfully sued the *Evening News* for
libel after they claimed his chess column contained blunders.

Ludwig Guttmann

Neurosurgeon and creator
of the Paralympics
1889–1980

Born into an Orthodox Jewish
family in Tost, Germany,
Guttmann was the son of an
innkeeper and distiller. He
studied medicine and worked
in neurology but when the
Nazis came to power Jewish doctors were forced to leave so-called
"Aryan" hospitals. Guttmann and his family moved to Oxford in
1939, where he worked in the Nuffield department of neurosurgery
at the Radcliffe Hospital. Guttmann was determined to refute
current thinking that those with severe spinal injuries and paralysis
could not be reintegrated into society. In 1944 he became the
manager of a new centre for the treatment of spinal injuries at
Stoke Mandeville in Buckinghamshire. He encouraged patients to
be as active and independent as possible and introduced sports
such as wheelchair basketball, table tennis and archery. On the day
of the opening ceremony of the London Olympics in 1948, Stoke
Mandeville hosted a wheelchair archery competition. This became
an annual event and soon an international competition with many
more sports included. This was the forerunner of the Paralympics
and by 2012 more than 4,200 athletes from 164 countries
competed in 20 sports. Guttmann was a founder of the British
Sports Association for the Disabled and was knighted in 1966.

Frederic Halford
Fly fishing pioneer
1844–1914

Frederic Hyam was born in Birmingham into a wealthy family. His father had a business mass-producing ready-made clothing. The family had moved from Germany generations earlier. When Frederic was seven they moved to London and he began fishing on the Serpentine. Upon leaving school he joined the family firm but by 1889 his love of fishing had become his passion and sole career. Hyam changed his name to Halford and moved to Hampshire where angling was a very popular sport. Dry-fly fishing was introduced in 1854 and Halford helped create a revolution in anglers' practices and ideas. Under his guidance anglers abandoned their silk and horsehair lines for dressed silk lines, which were less affected by strong winds. Further technological advances included improving the strength of rods by making them from split-cane and Halford came up with new ideas about efficient ways of fishing for trout in chalk streams. Known as the "High Priest of the Dry Fly", he wrote seven books including *Floating Flies and How to Dress Them* (1886) and *Dry-Fly Fishing in Theory and Practice* (1889). He also wrote for *The Field* magazine under the pseudonym "Detached Badger". Halford was buried at Willesden Jewish Cemetery in London.

Lewis Harris
Rugby player

Lewis Harris, also known as Louis Harris, was a English rugby league player. As a Jew he was part of the first significant minority group to play rugby in Britain. During the course of his career he played 255 matches for Hull Kingston Rovers scoring 76 tries and contibuting to the team's wins in the Northern Rugby Football Union Championships in 1921 and 1923.

Daniel Harrwitz

Chess master
1823 – 1884

Daniel Harrwitz was born in Breslau, then in the Prussian Province of Silesia. It was in Paris that his chess career began to flourish, and he gained a reputation as an accomplished player of blindfold games. In 1846 he lost a match in England to Howard Staunton, but had better luck in 1848 when he drew a match with Adolf Anderssen. In 1849 Harrwitz moved to England, where he founded the periodical the *British Chess Review*. He moved to Paris in 1856 and promptly won a match against Jules Arnous de Rivière. In 1858 he played his final significant match against Paul Morphy. Although he had a negative record against the chess master, he was one of the few masters who beat Morphy with the black pieces. He won the first two games, but withdrew from the match pleading ill-health. Harrwitz retired to Bolzano, Italy, then in the Austro-Hungarian county of Tyrol.

Maurice de Hirsch
Horseracing Baron
1831–1896

Maurice, Baron de Hirsch was born in Hamburg. He was the son of a banker whose family had been awarded a Bavarian barony in 1818. He worked for a Jewish bank in Brussels, marrying the owner's daughter, and then became a large-scale merchant banker in his own right. He was involved especially in Turkish finance and railway building. The most famous project that Hirsch financed was the construction of the *Orient Express* railway. In England, he often worked closely with the millionaire banker Sir Ernest Cassel. He lived at Bath House on Piccadilly, and was (like other wealthy Jewish financiers) a friend of the Prince of Wales. Hirsch was a keen racegoer, enjoying the society and the sport alike. He was a powerful patron of the Sport of Kings, and a wealthy owner of horseflesh. Hirsch is remembered for his philanthropy towards Europe's impoverished Jews, helping, especially, to promote Jewish immigration to Latin America. He is said to have given all his considerable race winnings to good causes, claiming that his horses ran for charity. He was an opponent of early Zionism, although he died a year before the first Zionist Congress. Hirsch was said to be worth more than £16m, and left £1.4m in England.

Philipp Hirschfeld
Chess master
1840–1896

Philipp Hirschfeld was born in Konigsberg, Prussia, into an affluent family. He learned chess as a child. In 1859, when he went to Berlin for his education, he was already a formidable player. He was also a strong chess theoretician, and worked in the editorial department of the chess periodical Deutschen Schachzeitung, where he published his analyses of opening theory. During his time in Berlin he played several high-profile matches before returning home to join his father's business. He moved to London to found the Konigsberg Tea Company, opening branches in Konigsberg, Moscow and China. On his travels he met and played with the greatest chess players of the day. He played individual games against Johann Jacob Lowenthal, Cecil de Vere and fellow Jews Bernhard Horwitz, Daniel Harrwitz and Wilhelm Steinitz. In 1864 he travelled to Paris to face one of the acknowledged chess champions in Europe, Ignaz Kolisch, in a good-natured battle. In 1873 he moved to London permanently, teaming up with analysis partner and Jewish chess master Johannes Zukertort.

Leopold Hoffer

Founder and editor of *Chess Monthly* magazine
1842–1913

Leopold Hoffer was born in Budapest, Hungary. From Budapest he moved to Switzerland, settling in Paris in 1867. There he won chess matches against some of the greats of the game. He defeated Ignatz von Kolisch, Samuel Rosenthal and Jules Arnous de Rivière before moving to England in 1870 and making his home in St Pancras, London. He continued to take on chess masters, losing to the American George Gossip in 1873 and then defeating James Minchin in 1876. One of Hoffer's greatest achievements was his victory over fellow Jew and Polish chess master Johannes Zukertort at London in 1887. Zukertort had narrowly missed out on the World Chess Championship the previous year. Outside of his playing career, Hoffer became increasingly involved in chess literature. Together, he and Zukertort in 1879 founded and edited the *Chess Monthly* magazine, which ran until 1896. Hoffer moved to Fulham in his later years, initially in a shared house with five other occupants, then in his own home in Glynn Mansions, where he lived with his niece Fren Reusz.

Bernhard Horwitz
Expert on endgames who
wrote *Chess Studies*
1807–1885

Bernhard Horwitz was born
in Neustrelitz, Germany. He
studied art at school in Berlin
and there became part of the
Berlin Pleiades, a group of rising
German chess players. The
group included chess masters and theoreticians Paul Rudolf von
Buelger and Tassilo von Heydebrand und der Lasa, who authored
the essential chess openings reference book, *Handbuch*. Horwitz
considered himself a member of the group until 1843. He moved to
London two years later but often struggled against the masters of
the game. Horwitz played German chess master Lionel Kieseritzky in
an epic match in 1846, losing 7.5–4.5 across the 12 games. The pair
drew the last game, which featured 67 moves. The same year, Horwitz
managed to defeat Howard Staunton, one of England's strongest
players, in four games. Horwitz entered the London Tournament
of 1851 and defeated Henry Bird in the first round, one of the
best results in his playing career. Horwitz was also an important
writer on the game and worked alongside Josef Kling to produce
the influential work *Chess Studies*, which they published in 1851.
Together they contributed a great deal to the study of endgames.

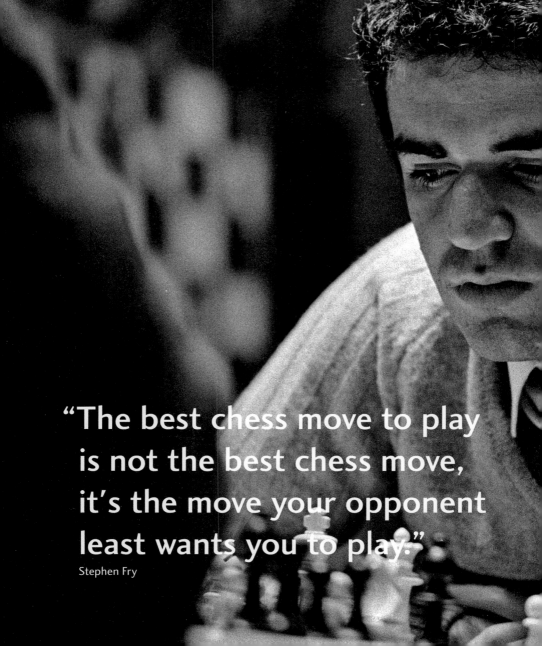

"The best chess move to play
is not the best chess move,
it's the move your opponent
least wants you to play."
Stephen Fry

British Jews in Chess

Since 1886 there have been sixteen undisputed
and official World Chess Champions. Of these
six (40%) of them have been Jewish. A seventh,
Gary Kasparov, pictured, rated the best chess
player of all time, has a Jewish father.

Jonathan Speelman, Grandmaster chess player, 1990

British Jews in Chess

John Lewis

Writer, Editor and Journalist

"Well, Jonathan, you've outplayed me, you've out-thought me, you've
humiliated me, and you've destroyed me," said Stephen Fry, after
a game of chess with the British grandmaster Jonathan Speelman.
"You've all but cut off my penis. Well done." This showdown came
as part of a 1990 TV documentary that Fry was making about the
Chess Olympiads – the Olympics of chess. It didn't go unremarked
that the documentary featured two British Jews playing each other at
a game that has been dominated by Jews for more than a century.

There have been Jewish men and women who have reached the
pinnacle of their sport –boxers, footballers, baseball players, middle-
distance runners – but there have been few sports where Jews have
been quite so heavily represented as in chess. Of the first dozen
undisputed world champions to emerge in the late 19th century and
early 20th century, more than half were Jewish. In the 21st century,
around a third of the top ten and around 28 per cent of the top
100 chess players are Jewish. Bat-Sheva in Israel has the highest
concentration of chess grandmasters, per capita, in the entire world.

According to Professor Arpad Elo's scientific ranking system, half
of the top 50 greatest chess players of all time have been Jewish.
They include the strongest player of all time, Garry Kasparov (the
Armenian-Russian who was undisputed champion between 1985 and
2005) and the great white hope of American chess Bobby Fischer
(who defeated the Soviet champion Boris Spassky in a 1972 contest
in Iceland that seemed to symbolize the Cold War). It includes the

great Mikhail Tal, the hard-living Latvian eccentric who famously declared that chess is about "taking your opponent into a deep dark forest where 2+2=5, and the path leading out is only wide enough for one." It includes literally dozens of world champions of the last century: Viktor Korchnoi, Emanuel Lasker, Mikhail Botvinnik, Levon Aronian, Boris Gelfand, Ilya Gurevich, Alexander Khalifman, Maxim Rodshtein, Wilhelm Steinitz and Peter Svidler. The greatest female chess players of all time, Judit and Susan Polgar, are Hungarian Jews.

Not all of these players have been practising Jews, of course. Botvinnik was a Marxist and atheist, Kasparov identified with his Christian Armenian mother's faith, while Fischer, though ethnically 100 per cent Jewish, was a profound antisemite. "There are too many Jews in chess," said Fischer, in one of his more outrageous outbursts. "They seem to have taken away the class of the game. They don't seem to dress so nicely. That's what I don't like."

But still, people have been remarking on this extraordinary relationship between Jews and chess for more than a century. The 1905 *American Chess Bulletin* described chess as "the Jewish national game", while a newspaper article on a 1911 chess championship observed that, of the 26 competitors, no fewer than half were Jewish. "The rivalry on strictly logical lines characterizing the game of chess, and the scope for ingenuity it affords make, we fancy, a special appeal to the Jewish temperament," wrote the article. "One has barely met an individual of that race who did not display at least some intelligent appreciation of the game."

Dozens of books, articles and academic studies have attempted to explain this affinity. Nathan Lopes Cardozo, the Dutch-Israeli rabbi and philosopher, claims that chess shares with the Talmud "a merciless, ruthless inflexibility". "Chess reminds Talmudic scholars, consciously or subconsciously, of the world of Talmudic halachic debate, with all its intrigues, obstacles and seemingly deliberate tendency to make life more difficult." Writing in his 1918 book *The Parallel Progress of Chess And Civilisation*, the French grandmaster Alphonse Goetz remarked that "the Israelish (sic) element has exercised a predominance out of all proportion to the number and position of the Jews," going on to suggest that: "The branches of activity are well known in which the Israelites have excelled for so long, and, as it were, by the force of atavism – banking, business, industry. In chess their supremacy began to manifest itself scarcely two generations ago. It has not ceased to grow stronger and stronger since then."

While it has been Jews of Eastern Europe and the former Soviet Union who traditionally dominated chess throughout much of the 20th century, they have also been a notable presence in the British game. Two of the most high-profile British chess grandmasters of recent years have been Jewish: broadcaster and one-time British champion William Hartston (now best known to UK TV audiences as one of the stars of Channel 4's *Gogglebox*), and Jonathan Speelman, three times British champion chess and chess columnist for the *Observer* and the *Independent*. Another Jonathan, the professor of applied mathematics Jonathan Mestel (born 1957), was the first chess player to be awarded grandmaster status by the World Chess Federation FIDE (Fédération Internationale des Échecs) for both his tournament play and his problem-solving skills, while the grandmaster Michael Stean (born 1953) was a British champion who worked closely with the Soviet Viktor Korchnoi. But Britain has been home to many Jewish chess stars going back more than two centuries.

From the 19th century onwards, there were many chess players among the Jewish intellectuals from Continental Europe who ended up in London. Aaron Alexandre (1766-1850), born in Germany and

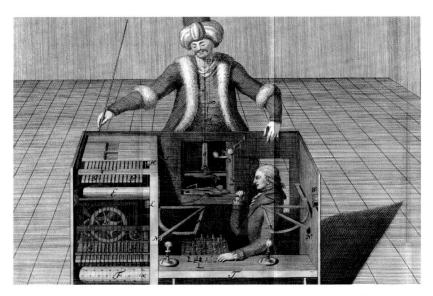

The Mechanical Turk, illustration explaining the illusion behind the chess playing automaton, known as The Mechanical Turk, 1789.

Johann Löwenthal, Lowenthal playing 21 year old American chess prodigy Paul Morphy in London, 1958.

raised in France, was already a known figure in the chess world when he emigrated to London in the late 1830s. He had published the *Encyclopedia of Chess* in 1837: translated into four languages, it was one of the earliest books to analyse chess openings and formulated the algebraic notation now commonly used in chess literature. While in London Alexandre wrote *The Beauties of Chess*, which contained 2,000 problems. He was also one of the secret operators of The Mechanical Turk, an automaton which toured Europe playing chess games against unsuspecting opponents who believed that they were playing against a machine. Alexandre was one of the top chess players who would hide inside the machine, carrying out moves on behalf of the beturbaned robot.

Alexandre was followed by other Jewish émigrés in London. Edward Löwe (1794-1880), born in Prague, came to London in the 1840s, and beat some of Britain's top international players, including Howard Staunton and Hugh Alexander Kennedy. Bernard Horwitz (1807-1885) was born in Germany and was part of a group of rising German chess players who called themselves the Pleiades. In 1845 he relocated to London where he defeated Staunton as well as another top British player, Henry Bird. In 1851 he and his fellow German expat Josef Kling (1811-1876) wrote *Chess Studies*, one of the first books studying the endgame.

It has often been British Jews who have served as interlocutors for chess – explaining this arcane game to newcomers, beginners and newspaper readers through books and articles. One of them was Johann Löwenthal (1810-1876). Born in Budapest, he was the son of a merchant who was expelled from Hungary in the 1850s and, after a spell in the US, ended up in England. He defeated the world chess champion Adolf Anderssen in 1857 and became the chess correspondent for the *Illustrated News Of The World*, set up *Chess*

Players Magazine between 1863 and 1867, and served as manager of the British Chess Association between 1865 and 1869. He converted to Catholicism late in his life under the influence of his close friend and chess sparring partner William George Ward.

Two other players also came to the UK from Budapest. Isidor Gunsberg (1854-1930) moved to London in 1876, and nearly won the world title in 1891, narrowly losing to the great Wilhelm Steinitz in 1891. There was also Leopold Hoffer (1842-1913), who lived in Switzerland and France before moving to London in 1870. Like Löwenthal, Hoffer also diversified into journalism, editing *Chess Monthly* between 1879 and 1896.

Hoffer's most famous victory came against the Polish-born Johannes Zukertort (1842-1888), who was probably the greatest Anglo-Jewish chess player of the 19th century. In January 1886 Zukertort – by this point Britain's top player – travelled to the United States to face the world's first undisputed chess champion, Wilhelm Steinitz, over the course of three months. After five matches in New York, Zukertort was 4-1 up but, as the pair resumed the contest in St Louis and then New Orleans, his health suffered and he ended up losing 12½–7½. He never really recovered from his illness in the States and died in June 1888 – suffering a cerebral haemorrhage during a tournament in London – at the age of only 45.

Throughout the 20th century more chess-playing Jewish émigrés arrived in Britain. Victor Buerger (1904-1996) was born in Ukraine but came to London in the 1920s: at a tournament in Margate in 1937 he even beat the great Alexander Alekhine – at that point the greatest chess player who had ever lived. Ernest Klein (1910-1990) was born in Vienna and moved to London in 1930, pushing some of the world's great grandmasters during his competitive career and eventually winning the British championship in 1951. Paul List (1887-

1954) came from Odessa in Ukraine, moved to Germany in the 1910s was one of the world's top ten chess players throughout the 1920s and 30s. He fled to Britain in 1937 to escape the Nazis, as did Imre König (1901-1992), a refugee from Hungary, who ended up as one of the world's top players throughout the 40s and 50s. Raaphi Persitz (1934-2009) was born in Tel Aviv and settled in Oxford in the early 1950s; David Friedgood (born 1946) arrived from South Africa in 1978.

Of course, by this time there were many British-born Jews competing at the top level in chess tournaments. Victor Wahltuch (1875-1953) was born in Chorlton-on-Medlock, Manchester and took part in many Lancashire v Yorkshire matches before settling in London. Baruch Harold Wood (1909-1989) was born in Sheffield and was a strong tournament player. He founded *Chess* magazine in 1935, serving as its editor until 1988, and also served as the *Daily Telegraph*'s chess correspondent. Then there was Harry Golombek (1911-1995) – born in the East End of London, he was a brilliant mathematician who served at Bletchley Park during the Second World War (where he would often play, and beat, Alan Turing at chess) before winning three British chess championships in the 1940s and 50s. He had a chess column in the Observer and published *The Game Of Chess* (1954), one of the best beginners' guides to the game.

Gerald Abrahams (1907-1980), a Liverpool-born chess champion and barrister, was one of Britain's finest players between the 1930s and the 1960s, defeating the Soviet grandmaster Viacheslav Ragozin in a 1946 tournament. He also wrote widely on chess, with bestselling guides including *Teach Yourself Chess* (1948), *The Chess Mind* (1951) and *The Pan Book Of Chess* (1966). In a 1973 essay he pondered why Jews were so predominant in chess. "My own theory is that Jews, through evolutionary processes, have become good at languages," he wrote. "To be good at languages it is desirable to reach maturity early, and grasp the accidence and syntax and important vocabulary at an early age, so that while the mind is still young the student can express himself fluently and with mastery."

Stephen Fry and Jonathan Spellman also briefly discussed this issue in their 1990 documentary on FIDE, linking prodigious talent in chess with talents in language, mathematics and music and suggesting that the game's theatrical fusion of all three disciplines seemed to be uniquely suited to a certain Jewish temperament. Fry's love of chess, he has said, is due to its intellectual purity and its complete lack of any practical application. "The fact is that chess is completely pointless," he says. "As Raymond Chandler so rightly said, it is the greatest waste of human intelligence outside an advertising agency."

Opposite Isaac Israëls, *The Chess Players*, 1900

"He was a powerful man,
over six feet in height ...
a supreme artist, revelling
in his triumphs and laughing
at his failures."

R. C. Robertson-Glasgow, Scottish cricketer and cricket writer

Biographies I – L

Dar Lyon was described by Wisden Cricketers'
Almanack as "among the best batsmen who never
gained a cap for England". In 1924 he was selected
to play for "The Rest" against England, in a three-
day Test Trial match, Lyon recorded scores of 32
and 3, and took a catch in both innings as wicket
keeper. He was the only member of the team not
to go on to represent England at Test cricket.

Harry Jacobs
Boxing promoter
1868–1929

Harry Jacobs began his career in promotion at the old Wonderland Hall in London's East End, and rose to the level of staging events in the Albert Hall in Kensington. In his time Harry Jacobs staged some of the most important boxing matches in the world, and became known in the boxing world as the "Rickard of Great Britain", a comparison to the American boxing promoter Tex Rickard. He suffered a period of bankruptcy but was soon back on top, placing the 16-year-old Jack "Kid" Berg at the top of his first Albert Hall bill, to face Harry Corbett in the ring. The bout was to determine which of the two in-form young men would face featherweight champion Johnny Curley. Of his stellar career the *Daily News* wrote "It needed a masterful personality to sway the unruly elements which made up the boxing game then, and Harry Jacobs never failed to rise to the occasion." Jacobs died a month after the new British Boxing Board of Control was endorsed.

Peter Jaffe
Sailor
1913 – 1982

James Peter Jaffe was born in Richmond, Greater London. He was a competitive sailor. At the 1932 Summer Olympics in Los Angeles, at the age of just 18, he won a silver medal. His craft was the mixed two-person keelboat, a small to midsize recreational sailing yacht with a flat bottom. He competed in the Star class, for boats weighing at least 671 kg with a maximum sail area of 26.5 metres square. The class requires the crew to adopt the extreme 'hiking' position, using a harness to hang low off the windward side of the boat with only their lower legs inside.

Jack Barnato Joel
Racehorse owner and breeder
1862–1940

Jack Barnato Joel was born in London. His father, Joel Joel, was the landlord of the King of Prussia tavern, and his mother was Kate Isaacs, sister to diamond magnate Barney Barnato. Barnato took Joel and his brothers under his wing, and taught them the diamond trade in South Africa. In 1882 Joel was accused of illicit diamond buying and detained, but his release was secured by Cecil Rhodes. Returning to London, he began to breed thoroughbred racehorses, registering his colours of "black jacket, scarlet cap". In 1903 Joel won the Oaks with his horse Our Lassie, and he repeated the feat in 1907 with Glass Doll. In 1908 he won the St Leger Stakes with his horse Your Majesty. Sunstar won the Derby in 1911 in the presence of the king and queen. In 1913 Jest won the Oaks again for him, and in 1914 Joel's horses managed a double: Princess Dorrie won the Oaks, and Black Jester raced to victory in the St Leger. Joel donated £1,000 of his winnings – then a considerable sum – to charity. In 1921 his horse Humorist came second in the Derby. Joel's great wealth saw him settled comfortably in St Albans, Hertfordshire. His house, Chidwickbury Manor, was purchased after his death by film director and fellow Jew Stanley Kubrick.

Solomon Joel
Racehorse owner and breeder
1865–1931

Solomon Joel was one of
three sons of Joel Joel, tavern
keeper of the King of Prussia
public house, and his wife Kate
Isaacs. In the 1880s Solomon
moved to South Africa with
his brothers Jack and Woolf to
make his fortune in diamonds, under the guidance of their uncle
Barney Barnato. Within ten years, Solomon was a millionaire; and
on Barnato's death in 1897 Joel became head of Barnato Brothers,
the family business. He ploughed a good portion of his wealth into
his great love – horseracing. He established a stud at New Farm,
near his own Berkshire estate. He owned Polymelus, a leading sire
in Great Britain and Ireland. Racing was a family affair for the Joels.
Solomon had a long-running rivalry with his brother, but never quite
matched Jack's success with his Derby winners Sunstar and Humorist.
His daughter Eileen became the first woman jockey to win an open
race, riding Hogier to victory in the Town Plate at Newmarket. The
Joel Stakes at Newmarket is named in Solomon Joel's honour.

"Young" Aschel Joseph
Welterweight boxing champion
1885–1952

Aschel Joseph was born in Aldgate, London, to a Russian-Jewish immigrant family. He was educated at the Jews' Free School, and learned to box at the Jewish Lads' Brigade. In 1903 he began boxing professionally. After an early winning streak in 1905 he claimed the English lightweight title following a draw with Alf Reed. In 1908 he beat Corporal Bill Baker and added the English welterweight title to his roster. In 1910 Joseph suffered a setback when he lost to Harry Lewis in a world welterweight title fight in Whitechapel. But that same year he redeemed himself in Paris, where a victory over "Battling" La Croix won him the European welterweight title. He only kept the title for a year, losing to Georges Carpentier in 1911. It was the beginning of a run of bad luck. In a non-title fight soon afterward Joseph lost to Arthur Evernden after being disqualified for holding in the third round. By 1912 he had lost his British title too, and resigned his Lonsdale belt.

Leon Joseph
The Wizard on the Wing
1920–1983

Leon Joseph was an amateur footballer who became a local hero. Joseph served in the Second World War, and employed his footballing skills playing on the army team. He sustained a leg injury when he was hit with a piece of shrapnel, and was told he would never play again. However, he recovered from the wound and after the war was scouted for Tottenham and West Ham. He was capped 13 times for the England amateurs. He played at Leytonstone Football Club in the 1940s and 50s. Joseph ran a menswear shop in Leytonstone High Road, but he refused to give up the business to turn professional, as the money wasn't good enough. Instead he became an idol to the people of Leytonstone who packed the Granleigh Road ground to see "The Wizard on the Wing". Resident Roy Dart remembers: "if we couldn't afford to get in, we used to pay to go up on to the platform at Leytonstone High Road station to watch from there." A memorial to Joseph is now on display in the Walnut Tree pub in Leytonstone High Road.

Ernest Klein
British Chess Champion who challenged the greatest players 1910–1990

Ernest Klein was born in Vienna, Austria. His family was Jewish with German and Hungarian ancestry. Klein moved to the United Kingdom in 1930 and began playing tournament chess. His first entry was at Gyor, Hungary in 1930. Klein drew his first two games with Janos Balogh and Herman Steiner, then defeated Erno Gereben and L. Reich. A further two draws and a victory came before Klein fell to two defeats and finished tied third–fourth overall. Klein came up against some of the greatest players of the game during his career. At Paris in 1935 he played the Polish and French chess grandmaster Savielly Tartakower, losing two games. In a rematch during the 1951 Staunton Memorial, Klein was victorious. Klein competed at Margate in 1935 and tied for fourth–fifth place after drawing with German grandmaster Jacques Mieses and American grandmaster Samuel Reshevsky. Klein was a trainer for world chess champion Alexander Alekhine during his 1935 match with Max Euwe. Klein had an unofficial role, helping Alekhine with analysis during the game before being forced to leave the playing-hall during the 28th game after an altercation with officials. Klein's greatest success came in 1951 when he won the British Championship.

Jack Koffman

Footballer

1920–1977

Jack Koffman was a left winger for Prestwich and England. In 1945 he moved from Northwich Victoria to the big league, signing for Manchester United. He was transferred to Hull City the following year, making four appearances for the club. In 1947 he moved from Congleton Town to Oldham Athletic, where he made three appearances.

Imre König

International Master
who competed at three
Chess Olympiads
1901–1992

Imre König was born in Gyula,
Hungary. He made his mark
in 1921 when he competed in
a chess tournament at Celje
and took second place. He
played a number of tournaments in Vienna over the rest of the
year, with a highest finish of third. König competed at Rohitsch-
Sauerbrunn in 1929, finishing in 12th place in a tournament won
by the Polish grandmaster Akiba Rubinstein. He tied for 2nd–4th
at Belgrade in 1937. König represented Yugoslavia at three Chess
Olympiads. At Prague in 1931 he won five games, drew two and
lost one. He also won five games at the sixth Chess Olympiad at
Warsaw in 1935, and seven during the unofficial Chess Olympiad
at Munich in 1936. König settled in England in 1938 and put in an
impressive performance at Bournemouth in 1939 to tie for fourth–
fifth, defeating fellow Jewish player Gerald Abrahams as well as the
German grandmaster Jacques Mieses. König finished fourth in 1948
at London. He played at the Hastings International Chess Congress
in 1948–9, finishing in second place behind the Russian grandmaster
Nicolas Rossolimo. König became an international master in 1951.

Walter Korn
Chess writer
1908–1997

Walter Korn was born in Prague, then in Czechoslovakia. He fled the worsening political situation in his homeland and came to London in 1939. He is known to have played a 13-year-old Gordon Crown, as an account appeared in the April 1943 issue of *Chess* magazine. After the Second World War he served as director of the U.N. Relief and Rehabilitation Administration, an organisation charged with the relocation of survivors of the concentration camps. In 1948 he was appointed director of World ORT, a non-profit global Jewish organisation that promotes education and training in worldwide communities. In 1950 he moved to the United States, settling in Detroit, where he worked at the Jewish Community Center as a business manager. He acted as a FIDE International Judge for chess competitions, and in 1972 contributed the entire topic of chess to the *Encyclopaedia Britannica*. For his writings Korn enlisted the help of top players such as grandmasters Larry Evans and Nick de Firmian. Korn's magnum opus was *Modern Chess Openings*, a work that has run to 13 editions, and is still considered essential reading for chess players at tournament level.

Edward Lasker
Chess and Go player
1885–1981

Edward Lasker was born in Kempen in Prussia, then in the German Empire, now in Poland. He was educated in Breslau, where he learned chess from Arnold Schottlander. In 1909 he won the City Championship in Berlin. He continued his education in Charlottenburg, graduating from the technical college in mechanical and electrical engineering in 1910. In 1911 Lasker wrote his first chess book, *Schachstrategie*, which ran into several English and German editions. He moved to London before the First World War, then later to the U.S., the homeland of his mother, where he won five U.S. Open Championships. In 1924 he was invited to participate in a legendary "All Stars" chess tournament featuring Alexander Alekhine, Efim Bogoljubov, Capablanca and Jewish blindfold chess master Richard Reti. He played an extraordinary match with fellow Jew Emanuel Lasker that lasted 103 moves and changed endgame theory. Some years after this epic battle the two masters found they were related. In the March 1974 edition of *Chess Life* magazine Edward Lasker said: "I did not discover that we were actually related until he (Emanuel Lasker) told me shortly before his death that someone had shown him a Lasker family tree on one of whose branches I was dangling."

Edward Lawrence Levy
World record-breaking
weightlifter and Olympic judge
1851–1932

Born in London, Levy worked
for a Birmingham-based brewers
and also ran a Jewish school. He
won the first British Amateur
Weightlifting Championship
in 1891 at the age of 40.
In the same year he won an international amateur weightlifting
championship and competed against champions from Brussels,
Hamburg, England, Vienna, Italy and Berlin. The three-day event
consisted mainly of repetition and alternate pressing with 56 or 84
pounds in each hand. Between 1891 and 1894 Levy set a total of
14 world records. In 1896, at the first modern Olympics in Athens,
Levy was a judge on the international weightlifting jury. Levy was a
founder of the Amateur Gymnastics Federation of Great Britain &
Ireland. He was also active in Birmingham politics as a member of
the Conservative Party and a member of a Masonic lodge. He wrote
and published books on all aspects of his life including *The Midland
Conservative Club (1883 and After)* (1909), *The Autobiography of an
Athlete* (1913), *Birmingham Athletic Club, 1866–1916* (1916), *The
History of the Lodge of Israel, 1474, Warwickshire,* 2 vols. (1916 and
1924) and *Birmingham Jewry, 1870, Then; and 1929, Now* (1929).

Ted "Kid" Lewis
Boxer
1894–1970

Probably the greatest fighter to ever come out of Britain, British Boxing legend Ted "Kid" Lewis was born Gershon Mendaloff to cabinet maker Harris and wife Leah. The family lived in London's East End, where Gershon attended the Jewish Free School. In 1909 he began boxing as "Kid Lewis" at the Judaean School and Athletic Club, Whitechapel. When the Premierland venue was opened in 1912 he competed there in 35 matches. This venue was popular with Jewish audiences and Jewish boxers. In 1913 Ted Lewis became the British featherweight champion and, later that year, the European champion. He is best remembered for his career-long rivalry with Jack Britton. Lewis defeated Britton in 1915, winning the World Welterweight Championship in Boston. Eight months later Britton won the title back. Lewis took it again in 1917 but then lost the title once more to Britton in 1919. In 1920 Lewis was crowned both British and European Welterweight Champion and in 1921 he was named British Middleweight Champion. He was inducted into the International Boxing Hall of Fame in 1992. Lewis was the first boxer to wear a protective mouthpiece, in 1913.

Paul List
Tied first with Golombek in the
1940 London tournament
1887–1954

Paul List was born in Odessa,
Ukraine. He began his chess
career there and won the 1908
tournament in his hometown.
He had a strong record in
matches against greats of the
game. In 1910 he played a nine-game match with Grigory Levenfish,
the Russian chess grandmaster and Soviet champion, and drew with
four wins, four losses and one tie. The same year he came third at
Odessa behind the international master Boris Verlinsky. In 1912,
List competed in the seventh edition of the All-Russian Masters'
Tournament at Vilna. List finished in tied fourth place with the chess
master Ilya Rabinovich, losing out to the Czech champion Karel
Hromádka. List moved to Germany in the 1920s and maintained
his strong tournament showing, tying for seventh, sixth and fifth in
Berlin and at Frankfurt in 1930 tying for third. List settled in Britain
in 1937. His performances continued to improve, and in 1939 he tied
for second at Birmingham and fourth in Hampstead. His greatest
achievement was in 1940 when he tied for first place with Harry
Golombek OBE at a London tournament. List came fifth in a
tournament at Zandam in 1946 won by grandmaster Max Euwe.

Rudolf Loman
Chess player
1861–1932

Rudolf Loman was born in Amsterdam. He was the son of Dutch theologian Abraham Dirk Loman. He won a number of unofficial Dutch championships, Rotterdam in 1888, The Hague in 1890, Utrecht in 1891, Groningen in 1893, a second victory in Rotterdam in 1894 and Utrecht again in 1897. Loman moved to London, and although he was an accomplished organ player and employed as a professional, he made a good living on the side playing chess for money against rich Englishmen. He trained his Dutch pupil, Jacques Davidson, to do the same. In 1904 he drew with Paul Saladin Leonhardt. On his return to the Netherlands he became Dutch chess champion in 1912. In 1913 he lost to Johannes Esser, and in 1922 to Edgar Colle.

Edward Löwe
Chess underdog who often
toppled the greats
1794–1880

Edward Löwe was born in Prague
in the historical Czech region
of Bohemia. He ultimately
settled in England, where he
played most of his competitive
chess. Löwe was something of
an underdog, a player with no ambitions of achieving the highest
rank but who, according to Chess Monthly, was often a "dangerous
opponent" for some of England's best talent. He proved as much
in 1847 when he defeated one of the greatest players of the game,
Howard Staunton, by five games to two, even though Staunton
had given Löwe a handicap of pawn and two moves. Löwe toppled
another giant in 1849 when he beat English chess master Hugh
Alexander Kennedy. He was less successful against Paul Morphy,
who beat him by six games to none at Löwe's hotel in London. Löwe
entered the 1849 London tournament, beating Arthur Simons by
two games to none before being knocked out by George Webb
Medley. Löwe joined the best chess players in Europe in the first
international chess tournament at London in 1851, won by Adolf
Anderssen of Germany. Löwe lost in the first round to Marmaduke
Wyvill, an English chess master and Liberal Party politician.

Johann Löwenthal

Chess master who defeated
the great Adolf Anderssen
1810–1876

Johann Löwenthal was born
in Budapest, Hungary. His
father was a Jewish merchant.
Löwenthal studied at Budapest
gymnasium. One of his earliest
recorded chess victories was
against Carl Hamppe, a Swiss-Austrian chess master and Austrian
government official. Löwenthal was appointed to a civil service role in
the revolutionary government of Lajos Kossuth in 1848. Löwenthal
was expelled from Hungary when the government was toppled,
and he relocated to America before settling in England. There
his chess career flourished and in 1857 he defeated international
champion Adolf Anderssen to finish first at the Manchester
tournament. He also became the chess editor at the Illustrated
News of the World. Löwenthal played the child prodigy Paul
Morphy at London in 1858, having previously lost twice to him in
America when the latter was only 12 years old. Morphy was again
victorious, but supposedly used his winning stakes of £100 to buy
Löwenthal a gift of furniture. Days later, Löwenthal won the British
Chess Association Congress in Birmingham, receiving a prize of
£63. He published a collection of Morphy's best games in 1860.
Löwenthal converted to Roman Catholicism in later life after being
introduced to the faith by his chess sparring partner W.G. Ward.

Hyman Lurie
Table tennis player
1918–1982

Hyman Lurie was from a family of Manchester Jews. His father, Israel Lurie, had a barber shop; the first in Manchester to serve women. Young Hyman later ran the shop for him. A prodigiously talented table tennis player, Lurie won a bronze medal, together with doubles partner Eric Filby, in the World Table Tennis Championships of 1938. In 1939 he went one better and won double bronze in the men's doubles tournament of the World Table Tennis Championships, this time partnering Ken Hyde. He was also selected for the Swaythling Cup, a men's team event. The cup itself was donated in 1926 by Lady Baroness Swaythling, mother of Jewish player Ivor Montagu.

Beverley Lyon
Cricketer
1902–1970

Bev Lyon was born into a family of Jewish origin in Surrey, England. He was a right-handed batsman who played for Oxford University and captained Gloucestershire. Lyon played 267 first-class matches in his career, scoring 10694 runs and taking 52 wickets. His highest score was 189. Lyon achieved a certain notoriety for his outspoken views on the sport and unorthodox style of captaincy. When county cricket was going through a rough patch in the late 1920s, Lyon proposed a new knock-out competition and Sunday cricket as a way of boosting interest in the game. It took 30 years before cricket officials deemed it acceptable to play cricket on the Christian Sabbath. Lyon loved a gamble, and in one game against Yorkshire told their captain that he would pay their side £5 for every six they hit in the innings. He took it upon himself to deliver exciting games of cricket for both participators and spectators, once bending the rules of the game to play a one-innings match against Yorkshire after the first two days were rained off. Lyon was Wisden Cricketer of the Year in 1931 after his innovative captaincy helped Gloucestershire to second place in the division.

Dar Lyon

Scored a century
against New Zealand
1898–1964

Dar Lyon was born into a
family of Jewish origin in Surrey,
England. He was educated
at Rugby School, where
he captained the eleven in his
final year. Lyon was a second
lieutenant during the First World War and returned in 1919 to study
at Trinity College, Cambridge, but his first-class debut was actually
against the Cambridge University Cricket Club after he was selected
for Somerset in May 1920. He scored his first first-class century
for Somerset in only his second game, against Worcestershire. Lyon
earned his blue the following year and represented Cambridge in
eight matches, including the Varsity game with Oxford when he
kept wicket. He scored more than 1,000 runs for Somerset in 1923,
earning him a spot in a Test Trial match against the England team
in 1924. He was the only player in the game who did not eventually
play for England, to the surprise of his contemporaries. Indeed,
Wisden described him as "among the best batsmen who never
gained a cap for England". He made his career-best score in 1923,
with a knock of 219 against Derbyshire. Lyon played for the MCC
in 1927, scoring a century against the New Zealand national team.

"You know sometimes football turns on the slightest biscuit of good fortune."

David Pleat

People of the Ball:
Football and British Jews

Albert Goodman, centre, was one of the earliest Jewish professional footballers in Britain playing in the 1919-20 Tottenham Hotspur side.

Tottenham Hotspur squad, 1953, Micky Dulin seated front row, third left

People of the Ball: Football and British Jews

Joanne Rosenthal
Writer, Editor and Journalist

"I am now convinced that the Jews have taken
up soccer in a most whole-hearted way."
Trevor Wignall, *Daily Express*, 1934

In an interview with the *Jewish Chronicle* in November 1979,
former Tottenham Hotspur footballer Micky Dulin expressed
frustration at what he saw as the Jewish community's lack of
interest in taking sport seriously as a career option. "The average
Jewish boy doesn't want anything to do with athletics. I blame the
parents. All they want is for their boys to become doctors and
lawyers and nothing else."

Dulin enjoyed a professional career in the 1950s, long
before the creation of the Premier League and the subsequent
transformation of football into the global business phenomenon
that it is today. He played at a transitional time in the social
and economic life of British Jewry. In the decades that followed,
British Jews evolved into a predominantly middle-class community,
entering in large numbers into professions such as law, finance
and medicine.

Notwithstanding the validity of Dulin's opinions, his comments
highlight the close relationship between Jews' changing socio-
economic conditions and their engagement with sport. To fully
appreciate how and why Jews have engaged with football over time,
it is necessary to consider the wider story of Jews in Britain.

A largely unknown figure in British Jewish history, the first Jew to play football professionally in this country was Louis Bookman. Bookman's story was typical of the experiences of tens of thousands of European Jews at the time. Born in Lithuania in 1890, he was just a young child when his family migrated to Ireland, joining the mass exodus of Jews who left the former Russian Empire at the turn of the 20th century escaping poverty and pogroms.

Bookman was the first Jewish player to gain international honours (for Ireland) and his club career included spells at Bradford City, West Bromwich Albion and Luton Town. The son of a rabbi, Bookman was a natural sportsman, excelling at both football and cricket. He carved out a successful sporting career in spite of his religious parents' disapproval.

During his playing days, he changed his surname from Buchalter to Bookman, opting for a name that would be easier for his teammates to pronounce. They nicknamed him "Abraham", perhaps as a sign of affection or as an indication that his Jewishness marked him out as different.

Albert Goodman and David Harry Morris were of the same generation as Bookman. Both were born in the East End of London to immigrant parents and both enjoyed professional careers in the top flight of British football. Goodman played for Tottenham Hotspur and Charlton Athletic. Morris's club career included Swindon Town, Fulham and Millwall. A record-breaking goal scorer, Morris remains a legend at Swindon Town to this day. Despite being religiously observant, he did play on Saturdays, but bowed out when games clashed with the Jewish high holidays.

It is no accident that these three Jewish men – and many others like them – grew up to love the beautiful game. Bookman,

Goodman and Morris were raised during a time that saw football take on an important role in the Jewish community.

The Jewish communal establishment worried about the impact that the influx of impoverished, Yiddish-speaking, eastern European Jews might have on their status in wider society. Fears spread that the newly arrived immigrants would lead Jews to be viewed as different and foreign, and that antisemitism would likely follow. Out of these concerns, a movement grew, with the explicit purpose of "anglicising" these immigrants.

Starting in the 1880s, prominent members of the Anglo-Jewish elite founded youth clubs that set out to transform immigrant children into upstanding English citizens, steering them away from what they viewed as negative influences prevalent in the inner cities. Youth clubs, such as Stepney Jewish Lads' Club in London and Grove House Lads' Club in Manchester, offered activities and sports geared towards integrating Jewish children into wider British society.

Football, the game of the masses, was enthusiastically embraced as a way of keeping fit and healthy and "ironing out the Ghetto bend" – a phrase in common usage at the time. It was hoped that strengthening the children's physiques would go some way to subverting antisemitic stereotypes presenting Jews as weak, weedy and bookish.

In the eyes of the patrons of the youth clubs, football was particularly effective in inculcating "British" values of fair play and good manners. As one member of the Brady Street Club for Working Boys later reflected, "If you lost a football match, you learned to say 'well played' to your opponents and go on your way. No bitterness, no fighting and no arguments. We were told that was the way it had to be. Those lessons were priceless."

Tottenham Hotspur, modern kippah.

England vs Germany, German football supporters giving the Nazi salute during the international match against England at White Hart Lane, London December 1935.

This was a lesson that David Harry Morris would also have been taught. Born a short walk from the club's Whitechapel home, Morris was a Brady Street member before embarking on his career in professional football.

It didn't take long for Jews to fall in love with the national game. In "The Alien Child", a 1911 article for the Jewish World, Algernon Lesser, who worked for the Jewish Lads Brigade, wrote:

"Most non-Jews, and many of our own community also, would be astonished if they were to visit a Jewish boys' club on a Saturday evening and listen to the conversation which goes on among the members. The results of the games in the football league and the games that afternoon are most keenly discussed, and loud is the wailing and great the distress among supporters of "The Spurs" if Tottenham Hotspur have had to lower their colours".

Tottenham Hotspur's Jewish fanbase grew in the early 20th century, largely as a result of geographical convenience. As one supporter explained in a letter to the *Jewish Chronicle*:

"It was possible to be in synagogue until the end of Musaf [part of the morning prayer service], to nip home for a quick plate of lokshen soup, and then to board a tram from Aldgate to White Hart Lane. No other ground could offer such ease of access."

When White Hart Lane was chosen to host the controversial match between England and Germany in 1935 – the first international friendly since Hitler rose to power – press reports estimated that Tottenham's home support was roughly one-third Jewish. Footage of the game offers the incongruous sight of a swastika flag flying over the club's stadium.

Although Tottenham Hotspur have an established reputation as a "Jewish club", many teams developed large Jewish fanbases in the interwar years, primarily in the major urban centres where

Leslie Goldberg playing for Leeds United in 1939.

most Jews lived. Tottenham's closest rivals, Arsenal, have a similarly strong Jewish following that dates back to the growth of the Jewish community in north London.

Supporting a team means belonging to a wider community, transcending divisions of class, ethnicity or religion. Émigré publisher and Arsenal fan Ernest Hecht articulated a feeling shared by many first- and second-generation immigrants when he explained his attachment to his club: "If you are a stranger in a strange land, you've got to hang on to something, to support somebody."

A glance through Arsenal match programmes from the 1960s provides evidence of how the club nurtured their relationship with their Jewish fans. A message in a programme from September 1965 notifies fans that the kick-off for the next fixture has been moved to a later time "in order to assist our many Jewish supporters who will be observing Rosh Hashanah."

For Jewish football fans, it would have been a particular thrill to see a member of the Jewish community playing for their local team. Anthony Clavane – author of *Does Your Rabbi Know You're Here?*, which celebrates the Jewish pioneers of English football – has described the impact of seeing Leslie Goldberg breaking into the Leeds United squad on the club's Jewish supporters, his visibility making them feel part of the wider community.

Goldberg was a fast-paced right back and a favourite at Leeds United until his career was interrupted by the war. After signing for Reading in 1947, he changed his surname to the less conspicuous Gaunt in response to the antisemitism he experienced in the town.

While the number of Jews who have pursued careers in professional football has been modest, this might have been different under other economic circumstances. For some players,

Mark Lazarus playing for Queens Park Rangers, October 1962.

David Pleat, the Tottenham Hotspur manager with his England contingent of Chris Waddle, Gary Stevens and Glenn Hoddle at the 1986 World Cup Finals in Mexico.

the pressures of supporting a family meant that promising careers had to be abandoned. A maximum wage of £20 per week for players was in force until 1961, making professional football a precarious way to earn a living.

Leon Joseph began playing football in the East End of London at Oxford and St George's Boys Club and went on to become one of the most highly regarded amateur footballers of his day. In spite of several offers from top clubs, Joseph turned down opportunities to sign as a professional player, opting instead to move into the relative safety of the menswear business.

One of the best-known Jewish footballers is Mark Lazarus, who was born into a family of Jewish boxers in the East End. He gave up boxing as a schoolboy and pursued a career in professional football, playing for clubs such as Queens Park Rangers, Leyton Orient and Crystal Palace. Lazarus achieved hero status when he scored the League Cup-winning goal for Queens Park Rangers at Wembley in 1967.

Undoubtedly the most celebrated Jewish footballer in British history is David Pleat, a hugely well-established figure, whose career spans six decades. Pleat has had success in nearly every role the game has to offer – as player, manager, scout, commentator and journalist.

Pleat did not feel comfortable publicly acknowledging his Jewish identity until fairly recently, and yet his story is typical of the British-Jewish experience. Born in Nottingham in 1945, his family moved to Britain from eastern Europe, eventually anglicising their name from the Yiddish-sounding Plotz to Pleat. His father's love of football had been ignited during his days as a member of the Oxford and St George's Jewish Lads Club in Whitechapel.

In the second half of the 20th century, the Jewish community benefitted from social mobility and Jews gained entry into a wider range of professions. This development coincided with important changes in the football world as British football moved into an era of professionalism and enterprise.

A number of Jewish businessmen around the country enthusiastically seized the chance to participate at board level as directors and chairmen of the clubs they loved. As Michael Grade is quoted as saying, "What was there for Jews back then? Jewish outsiders got involved in football clubs because suddenly it was open to them."

Grade's father Leslie sat on the board of Leyton Orient under the chairmanship of Harry Zussman, a larger-than-life character who took the club to the First Division for the first time in their history. By the mid-1970s a strong Jewish presence was established in the boardrooms of Brighton and Hove Albion, Leeds United, Leyton Orient and Millwall, as well as many others.

This continued into the 1980s and 1990s with figures like Irving Scholar and David Bernstein becoming hugely successful chairmen of their boyhood clubs, Tottenham Hotspur and Manchester City respectively. Their impact was transformative. In the words of Arsène Wenger, former Arsenal Vice Chairman and lifelong fan David Dein "revolutionised not only Arsenal, but the whole of English football."

In 1992, England's top 22 clubs broke away from the Football League to form the Premier League in a move that has redefined English football. The founding of the new league was the result of years of negotiations led by key football figures including Dein and Scholar. After 100 years of participation as footballers and fans, British Jews had now become major players.

Opposite Harry Zussman, Leyton Orient vs Coventry, Brisbane Road, 1955.

"In the cold snow of Munich, they laid down their lives. But they live on forever in our hearts and our minds. So come all supporters and hold your heads high. For Manchester United will never die."

The *Flowers of Manchester*, official club memorial poem

Biographies M – R

Twenty-three people, including eight players of Manchester United football team and eight sports journalists, including Henry Rose of the *Daily Express*, were killed when their plane crashed after take off at the Munich-Riem airport on the 6th of February 1958.

Joshua Margoschis
Football chairman

Joshua Margoschis is thought to be the very first Jewish chairman of a British football club. He presided over Aston Villa when they won the League and Cup double in their magical 1896–7 season. He was a local tobacconist, and is remembered as one of the earliest examples of Jewish involvement in football at the level of the boardroom. He paved the way for future chairmen to lead clubs such as Leeds United, Arsenal, Celtic and Chelsea, the latter owned by fellow Jew Roman Abramovich.

Harry Mizler

Boxer
1913 – 1990

Hyman Barnett "Harry" Mizler was born in St Georges, in the heart of London's East End. His family had a fish stall in Watney Street Market, and Harry worked on the stall together with his brothers Moe and Judah. From 1929–30 he held the Federation of Working Men's Clubs bantamweight title. In 1930 he won the ABA bantamweight title. In the same year, at the age of just 17, he won the gold medal in the bantamweight class of the Empire Games in Hamilton, Canada. In the 1932 Los Angeles Olympic Games he was eliminated in the first round of the lightweight class. In 1934, on home turf, he was back on top once more when he defeated Johnny Cuthbert in 15 rounds for the Boxing Board of Control lightweight title at the Royal Albert Hall. Later that year, however, he lost the title to the much more experienced Jewish boxer Jack "Kid" Berg. After two further losses to Jimmy Walsh and Petey Sarron, Mizler tried his luck Stateside and defeated Sarron in a return bout. In 1940 Mizler was called up into the Royal Air Force and put his physical abilities to good use as a trainer, teaching young airmen the rudiments of boxing.

Moe Mizler
Boxer
1909–1999

Moe Mizler, older brother of champion boxer Harry Mizler, was born in Wicket Street, St Georges, in London's East End. The family owned a fish stall in Watney Street Market, and after leaving school Moe worked on the stall with his younger brothers Harry and Judah. He became a flyweight boxer, turning professional expressly to earn money to support the fish stall, perhaps encouraged by his father who was quoted as saying his sons could make "money, real money, punching the heads off of each other." Although he never reached the heights of his younger brother's boxing career, Moe nonetheless had several high-profile fights at Whitechapel's fabled Premierland venue, including bouts with Kid Rich, Nipper Pat Daley and Arthur Boy Edge.

Harry Morris
Footballer
1897–1985

David Hyman Morris, commonly known as Harry or Abe Morris, was born in Spitalfields, London. He was educated at the Jews' Free School and was a member of the Brady Street Boys' Club. During the First World War he served with the Middlesex Regiment. He began his footballing career as a handy goal scorer for Hackney Marshes side Vicar of Wakefield. He was scouted by manager Phil Kelso and signed for Fulham in 1919, leaving in 1921, when he joined Brentford. In the 1921–1922 season, he was top scorer, with 17 goals in 39 appearances. Morris retained the title in the following season, then signed for Millwall. By the time he left in 1925 he had scored 30 goals in 76 appearances. He signed to Swansea Town and stayed for one season, making just nine appearances. In June 1926 he signed for Swindon Town and made a great start, scoring hat-tricks in his first two matches. He went on to enjoy seven successful years at the club. In 2013 Harry Morris was voted Swindon Town's greatest ever player by the club's supporters. He remains the club's top goal scorer in a league match, season and career.

Daniel Mendoza
He showed Jews how
to fight back
1764–1836

Daniel Mendoza was born in
Horse Shoe Alley, east London
to a family of Portuguese-
Jewish descent. His father
was Abraham Mendoza, a tea
merchant, and his mother
was Esther Lopez. Daniel attended the Jewish School and then
worked with different tradesmen as a glass-cutter, fruiterer and tea
merchant. In 1789 Mendoza had his first professional fight and beat
Sam Martin the "Bath Butcher" in Barnet. This gave Mendoza the
reputation of a first-class fighter. He became the heavyweight
boxing champion of England between 1792 and 1795 and was a
celebrity in his time. He charged his seconds to carry two pigeons
to each fight, one black and one white. Mendoza would release the
white if he won, the black if he lost; a practice that only added to
his legend. Mendoza married his cousin Esther Mendoza and they
had 11 children. He opened an academy of fighting, teaching the
art of self-defence. Mendoza introduced new strategies of defence
and techniques that became the foundation of modern boxing. His
example as the first Jewish boxing champion encouraged young
Jews to fight and challenged the image of the weak Jew in society.
Mendoza himself was the first Jew to be presented to George III. The
comedian Peter Sellers was a direct descendant of Daniel Mendoza.

Jacques Mieses

Grandmaster who pioneered
the Mieses Opening
1865–1954

Jacques Mieses was born in
Leipzig, Germany. He could
compete with the chess greats
from a young age and at the age
of 17 he won the Berlin chess
championship. Five years later
he finished third at Nuremberg and joint second at Leipzig. His first
international tournament was the famous Hastings tournament of
1895, which brought together the best players of the day. Mieses
finished in 20th place, but he was determined to compete at the
highest level. Over a decade later in 1907 he won the inaugural
Leopold Trebitsch Memorial Tournament in Vienna. He also finished
third at Ostend the same year. In 1909, Mieses played future World
Championship contender Carl Schlechter in a blindfold match and
defeated him with two wins and a draw. Mieses organised the San
Sebastian tournament in 1911, which introduced the world to the
future champion Jose Raul Capablanca. In the 1930s, Mieses fled
Germany to escape Nazi persecution and settled in England, where
he became a naturalised citizen. He became a grandmaster in
1950, the first British player to be recognised with the title by the
World Chess Federation. The opening 1.d3 is named after Mieses.

Ivor Montagu

Champion of table tennis
and the people
1904–1984

Ivor Montagu was born into a
wealthy family in Kensington,
London. His father was a banker.
Ivor attended Westminster
School – at a time when Jews
were not allowed to board –
then read zoology at Cambridge. He was a lifelong Communist
and after visiting the Soviet Union in 1925 he worked for Anglo-
Soviet friendship. A champion table tennis player, he founded the
International Table Tennis Federation and the English Table Tennis
Federation. Previously the sport was played by the aristocracy;
Montagu turned it into a sport for the workers. One of the founders
of the London Film Society in 1925, Montagu brought Soviet cinema
to the screen. A devotee of Eisenstein, he travelled with him to
America, a trip that he later recounted in a memoir, *In Hollywood
with Eisenstein* (1968). He collaborated on many films and made
political documentaries criticising the indifference of politicians
such as Neville Chamberlain to the conditions suffered by the
poor. Montagu was film critic for the Observer and journalist on
the Daily Worker. He opposed the involvement of Britain in the 1936
Nazi-run Olympics in Berlin. Montagu founded the Association of
Cinematograph, Television and Allied Technicians (ACTAT) a union
for those involved in film and TV, which later became BECTU.

Fred Oberlander

Championship wrestler
and Olympic athlete
1911 – 1996

Fred Oberlander was born
in Vienna, Austria. His first
wrestling match was against a
German champion, Kurt Siebert.
Oberlander remembers how
sportswear became a political
issue: "The German coach objected to the Hakoah [of Vienna]
emblem on my wrestling attire, claiming that it was a political
insignia. I answered that it was my club's emblem, which it was.
Finally, the referee decided that the Swastika on Siebert's jersey
was also a political insignia. On that note, the match began — and
finished in my favour." Between 1930 and 1950 Oberlander won
two Austrian junior titles, five French heavyweight championships
and the 1950 Canadian heavyweight crown. In 1935 he was listed
as "stateless" at the World Championships. He was asked to
represent Austria at the 1936 Olympic Games in Berlin. "For obvious
reasons, being Jewish, I refused," Oberlander later commented. His
successes included wins at the World Exhibition Championship in
Brussels in 1935, the Moulin Rouge International Championships
in 1937, the Allied Championships in 1944 and the Commonwealth
Games in 1948. Oberlander was nominated British team captain
at the 1948 Olympic Games. When he emigrated to Canada,
Oberlander set up the Canadian Maccabi Association. In 1953
he became Maccabiah Games wrestling heavyweight champion
and was awarded the title Outstanding Jewish World Athlete.

Raaphi Persitz
Precocious chess player who
could memorise entire games
1934–2009

Raaphi Persitz was born in the
British Mandate of Palestine
in modern-day Tel Aviv, Israel.
He excelled at chess from a
young age, and his incredible
memory allowed him to recall
entire games as well as all the openings and endgames. Persitz could
comfortably keep up with several chess games simultaneously, and
often did so on the way to kibbutzim. He won the inaugural junior
edition of the Israeli Chess Championship in 1951. Persitz moved
to England for his education and studied economics at Balliol
College, Oxford. He represented Oxford at chess in the Varsity
match three times. He also played in the World Student Team Chess
Championship three times for England. In his first outing at Oslo
in 1954, Persitz won an individual gold medal. Persitz eventually
returned to Israel and represented his country in the 14th Chess
Olympiad at Leipzig in 1960, winning seven points from 12 games.
Persitz was a popular writer on the game and regularly contributed
to British Chess magazine. He also had a strong grasp of the Hebrew
language and was a member of the Hebrew Language Academy.
He wrote a number of articles for the Israeli newspaper Haaretz.

Daniel Prenn
Tennis player
1904–1991

Daniel Prenn was born in Vilnius, then part of Russia. His family fled the pogroms to Berlin. He attended Charlottenburg Technical High School and worked an after-school job at a sports shop. He was a successful boxer and played football and table tennis but the game at which he most excelled was tennis. A tenacious player and great strategist, he displayed an iron will to succeed. In 1929, the year Prenn graduated in engineering, he was ranked number one in German tennis, a position he held until 1932. He was declared "Europe's number one man" by American Lawn Tennis magazine and led the German team to its unlikely victory over England, beating the top seeds Fred Perry and Bunny Austin. In that same year he was ranked eighth in the world by the American tennis champion Bill Tilden. Prenn was barred from taking part in all competitions by the Nazis in 1933. The German Tennis Federation had passed a restriction that no Jew could be selected for the national team and that no Jew or Marxist could be affiliated to the federation or hold an official position. Prenn moved to Britain and became a British subject but never matched the success that he had enjoyed in Germany.

Samuel Rabin

Wrestler, singer, actor
and sculptor; all-round
Renaissance man
1903–1991

Samuel Rabin was born in
Cheetham, north Manchester,
to a family of Russian
exiles. The family name was
originally Rabinovitch. Aged
11, Samuel became the youngest student to win a scholarship to
the Manchester Municipal School of Art. He moved on to Slade
School of Fine Art in London. In 1928 Rabin was commissioned to
carve a stone sculpture for the London Underground headquarters
and in 1930 he produced sculptures for the front of the Daily
Telegraph building. Rabin had incredible physical strength and
competed as an amateur boxer and wrestler. He won a bronze
medal for middleweight freestyle wrestling at the Amsterdam
Olympics in 1928. When he turned professional in 1932 he took
part in fights across the country and called himself "Rabin the
Cat" and "Sam Radnor the Hebrew Jew". He caught the attention of
the film producer Alexander Korda, who cast him as the champion
wrestler in *The Private Life of Henry VIII* (1933) and as the Jewish
prizefighter Mendoza in *The Scarlet Pimpernel* (1934). During the
1940s he worked as a professional bass baritone singer, using the
name Samuel Rabin. In 1949 he taught at Goldsmiths› College of
Art in London and his pupils included the designer Mary Quant.
He won the 1977 International Biennale of Sport in Fine Art.

John Raphael

Captained the British
Lions in Argentina
1882–1917

John Raphael was born in
Brussels, Belgium. His father
was Albert Raphael, a member
of a banking empire that once
challenged the Rothschilds. John
studied at Merchant Taylors'
school. In 1902, he won his first cap for the England rugby team
in a Home Nations championship match against Wales. He was a
utility back, playing variously on the wing, at centre or as a full-
back. Raphael appeared for the national team again in the 1905
and 1906 championships as well as in fixtures against New Zealand
and France. He was the captain during the British Lions tour of
Argentina in 1910, which featured the first ever test match played by
the South American side. Raphael was also a specialist batsman and
represented both Oxford University and Surrey at cricket. He scored
five centuries during his career, including one double hundred for
Oxford against Yorkshire. His 201 is the highest score made by an
Oxford cricketer against Yorkshire. Raphael captained Surrey for most
of the 1904 County Championship and scored one century against
Worcestershire. He died of his wounds at the Battle of Messines in
1917 while serving as a lieutenant with the King's Royal Rifle Corps.

Henry Rose
Sports journalist
1899-1958

On 6 February 1958, the British European Airways Elizabethan class aircraft carrying the Manchester United team home from Belgrade crashed on take-off, killing 20 of the 44 people on board. Much has been said about the "Busby Babes", the young and talented football players who were lost that day. But another team died too – eight journalists who were among the finest football writers of the day. Henry Rose was a Jewish sports writer for the *Daily Express* newspaper. He was known as an irrepressible, larger-than-life-character, whose footballing prose was second to none. David Walker, sports editor of the *Daily Mirror*, said of Rose: "He drove to matches in his Jaguar car and his arrival in the press box, usually with a cigar jutting from his mouth, would be announced over the club PA system. At this time, the only United player with a car was skipper Roger Byrne, who drove a Morris Minor 1000." Rose was almost as revered by the Manchester public as the players they'd lost; his funeral procession stretched six miles to the Southern Cemetery, with a fleet of taxi drivers conveying mourners to the burial without charge.

Leopold de Rothschild
Thoroughbred racehorse owner
1845-1917

Leopold de Rothschild's parents were Lionel de Rothschild and Charlotte von Rothschild. He was educated at King's College School and Trinity College Cambridge, after which he entered N M Rothschild & Sons, the family business. Rothschild resided at Gunnersbury Park, a house that once belonged to Princess Amelia, daughter of George II. He became a pillar of the British Establishment – he regularly entertained his close friend H.R.H. Edward, Prince of Wales at Palace House in Newmarket, and the prince attended Rothschild's wedding at London's Central Synagogue. An avid sportsman, Rothschild established Southcourt Stud in Bedfordshire. His stable gained the reputation of having some of the best thoroughbreds in Europe, and they triumphed at The Derby, The St. Leger Stakes and the 2000 guineas. Rothschild's horses romped home in the Epsom Derby in 1879 and 1904, and he won 851 races during his career as an owner. On his death in 1917, the British racing press remembered him as one of their own, characterising him as a 'munificent turf patron.'

"…it ruins hundreds if not thousands of men, body and soul, mind and purse - yet I was sorry that Uncle Mayer did not carry off the laurels of the day."

Charlotte de Rothschild

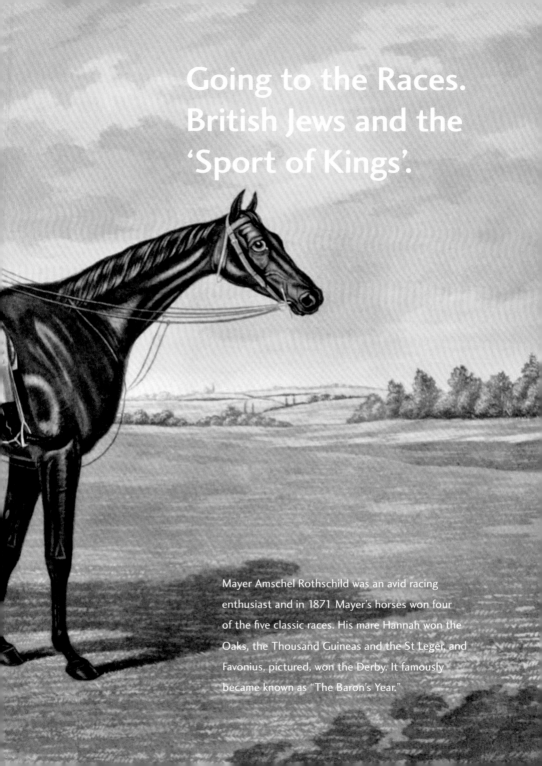

Going to the Races.
British Jews and the
'Sport of Kings'.

Mayer Amschel Rothschild was an avid racing
enthusiast and in 1871 Mayer's horses won four
of the five classic races. His mare Hannah won the
Oaks, the Thousand Guineas and the St Leger, and
Favonius, pictured, won the Derby. It famously
became known as "The Baron's Year."

Sir Victor Sassoon leads in his horse Crepello, ridden by Lester Piggott, winner of the 1957 Epsom Derby.

Going to the races.
British Jews and the 'Sport of Kings'.

David Bownes

Social Historian and Curator

By the mid nineteenth century, horseracing was firmly established
as the elite sport of royals and aristocrats popularly supported by
all classes of society. It was also a way into the upper echelons of
fashionable society for wealthy businessmen wishing to transcend
humble origins. Together with a country house and a passion for
'hunting, shooting and fishing', owning a stud of thoroughbred
racehorses was a mark of the English gentleman, theoretically
available to all who could afford the eye-watering price. Among those
hoping to achieve social acceptance in this way were the leading
Anglo-Jewish families, such as the Rothschilds, Sassoons and Cassels,
whose money had been made in trade and banking. Their close
association with horseracing, as owners and trainers, has been cited
as evidence of the openness of British high-society to outsiders,
and certainly resulted in several prominent English Jews entering
the private circle of the Prince of Wales (later King Edward VII). But
this enthusiasm for the sport was more than just a cynical ploy to
secure advancement. The Rothschilds, in particular, were known for
their sincere interest in racing matters, while the association between
the Baghdadi-Jewish Sassoons and the sport pre-dated the family's
arrival in Britain and continued well into the twentieth century. The
3rd Baronet, Sir Victor Sassoon, was especially fond of the English
season, purportedly declaring "there is only one race greater than
the Jews, and that is the Derby."

The entry of 'rich Jews' into the racing fraternity was not universally welcomed, however. The historian David Dee has shown how endemic antisemitism amongst some of the older aristocracy and gentry led to resentment towards wealthy Jews whose country homes and lifestyles were dismissed as "tasteless, vulgar, ostentatious and 'un-English'." Such resentment could effectively frustrate social ambition. With the exception of the Rothschild family, for example, none of the nineteenth century Jewish racehorse owners were afforded membership of the exclusive Jockey Club. The wider involvement of Jews with horseracing was also criticised in the popular press. Writing in 1881, the sporting correspondent of the *Glasgow Herald* lamented that "of late years the ranks of owners of horses have been strongly recruited from Jews", adding disapprovingly that track-side gambling "has no more enthusiastic supporters than the people of the ancient race". This alleged enthusiasm for gambling, coupled with the supposedly ubiquitous presence of untrustworthy Jewish bookmakers at race meets, was much repeated in plays and songs of the time and later used to recruit support for the British fascist movement in the 1930s.

The first major Anglo-Jewish racehorse owners came from the Rothschild banking family, which began to race horses competitively from the 1830s. The most prominent owner was Baron Mayer Amschel de Rothschild, the youngest son of the London bank's founder Nathan, who registered the Rothschild racing colours of dark blue and yellow in 1843. Like his older brothers, Mayer was a keen fox hunter and entering the world of racing would have seemed like a natural, and socially advantageous, progression. After establishing a stud farm at Crafton, near his country estate of Mentmore, Meyer moved his stable to Newmarket in the 1850s. He soon began to achieve considerable racing success and in 1871 Mayer's horses won four of the five 'Classics' (the Oaks, the Thousand Guineas, the St Leger, and the Derby) in what became known as 'The Baron's Year'.

His brothers Anthony and Lionel were also notable race-goers and thoroughbred breeders, with the latter owning a stud farm at Gunnersbury Park in west London. This was inherited by Leopold ('Leo') de Rothschild, who surpassed even his uncle Mayer's passion for racing. He won his first race, the Epsom Derby, in 1879, and established a very successful (and famously expensive) stable at Southcourt Farm on his Ascot estate. Leo's spiritual home, though, was said to be Palace House in Newmarket where he regularly entertained the Prince of Wales and other notable figures of the day. Despite winning an incredible 851 races during his career as an owner, including four Classics, the cost of running his stables ensured that Leo raced for love of the sport rather than profit – a trait which endeared him to the British racing public. At his death in 1917, the sporting press devoted many pages to his achievements, describing him as a 'munificent turf patron'.

As in so many aspects of Anglo-Jewish history, where the Rothschilds led other prominent Jewish families followed. In the 1880s the fabulously wealthy Munich banker and railway contractor Baron Maurice de Hirsh began to invest heavily in the English racing scene. Although he spent lavishly on horses, winning both the Oaks and St Leger in 1892, he gave all his racing profits to philanthropic causes, saying that his horses ran for charity. Like the Rothschilds, De Hirsh's involvement with the sport at the highest level bought him into contact with the British royal family and he, too, became a close friend of the Prince of Wales.

Another member of the Prince's inner circle drawn from the horse racing world was the Jewish banker and money-lender Sir Ernest Cassel. In time he came to replace De Hirsh as the Prince's closest male friend. Envious aristocrats referred contemptuously to the 'Windsor Cassels',

Prince Palatine owned by Jack Solomon wins the Coronation Cup at Epsom, 1913

Hurricane Run owned by Michael Tabor, ridden by Kieren Fallon, winner of both the Prix de l'Arc de Triomphe and the King George VI and Queen Elizabeth Stakes.

while Lady Paget complained that the Prince was "always surrounded by a bevy of Jews and a ring of racing people". Despite spending huge sums on his horses and stables at Newmarket, Cassel found little success on the race course. His story also reveals the difficulties faced by wealthy Jews wishing to assimilate into British society, even with royal patronage, and it is thought that his later conversion to Catholicism was an attempt to gain wider acceptance among the ruling elite.

Far more successful, in terms of sporting triumph, were the Joel brothers Jack and Solomon, who became the leading Jewish owners in the early twentieth century. The sons of an East End publican, the brothers made their fortunes in the South African diamond fields. Jack has been termed 'one of the last great English owner-breeders', and his horses won 504 races between 1900 and 1940, including eleven Classics. He was also known for his prodigious spending, paying the then record sum of £40,000 for one horse, *Prince Palatine*. The brother's racing legacy continued into the post Second World War era with their sons Harry, Jim and Stanhope taking over the reins of the family business.

Unlike the Joels and other Anglo-Jewish owners, the Sassoon merchant family had a long history of horse racing. With their origins in modern day Iraq, the family's business interests stretched to India, China and Hong Kong where the Sassoons were well-known for both breeding and jockeying race horses over several generations. The sport's most celebrated English supporter was the Shanghai businessman Sir Victor Sassoon, who purchased the Bungalow Stud near Newmarket in 1925. Renamed Eve Stud Ltd, and under the auspices of renowned trainer Sir Noel Murless, the stables became world famous and a source of numerous winners. Sir Victor continued racing until his death in 1961 with notable victories including the

Derby, St. Leger, King George VI and Queen Elizabeth Stakes. The First World War poet and author Siegfried Sassoon, who was descended through his father's side from the great mercantile family, was also an avid racing enthusiast, owning several horses which he raced and hunted himself. Ironically, Siegfried believed that he inherited his love of riding and hunting from his Anglican maternal ancestry, apparently unaware of the Sassoon racing tradition.

In more recent years, the businessman and philanthropist Michael Sobell forged an enviable reputation as a breeder of thoroughbred winners, with stud farms in Ireland and England. His greatest sporting success came in 1979 when his colt *Troy* romped to victory in the Epsom and Irish Derbies, the Benson & Hedges Gold Cup and the King George VI and Queen Elizabeth Stakes, earning Sobell the title of British Flat Racing Champion Owner. Other notable winners from the Sobell stud include *Admetus*, who won the Washington D.C. International Stakes in 1974, and *Sun Princess*, winner of the 1983 Oaks and the St. Leger.

Similarly, the gambling tycoon Michael Barry Tabor has enjoyed huge success on the British and international racing circuit with his stud of Irish and English trained horses. Acknowledged as the owner and co-owner of some of the world's best racehorses, Tabor is one of only four men to have raced a winner at both the Epsom and Kentucky Derbies. His famous stable included *Desert King* (winner of the Irish 2,000 Guineas and the Irish Derby in 1997), *Giant's Causeway* (winner of numerous Group One races) and *Hurricane Run* (voted the world's top-ranked racehorse by the International Federation of Horseracing Authorities, 1995).

Away from the rarefied world of owners and trainers, Jewish bookmakers played a significant (if sometimes exaggerated) role in running on-course gambling – the only licenced form of horse race betting in England until 1960. Their success in this field, however, was not without criticism. Professor Mike Huggins has argued that the negative portrayal of Jewish 'turf accountants' during the nineteenth and twentieth centuries drew on long established antisemitic tropes, which were frequently evoked in the press and by those who had lost more than they could afford. Hence, Jewish bookmakers were typically described as "greedier for money, less honest and more attracted to betting than other ethnic groups". There was also a deep-seated prejudice against the perceived 'parasitic' inclination of Jews to feed off the earnings of the British working man. In December 1921 the *Sporting Times*, for example, reported overhearing a "well known Jewish bookmaker" glumly reflecting on an apparently profitable day's racing at Kempton: "how do these ruddy Christians get all the money we take from them?".

Theoretically, at least, Orthodox Jewish teaching strongly disapproved of gambling of any sort, and it was noted at the time that Jewish bookmakers were less in evidence on the Sabbath. But even this observance could be turned against them. After several outsiders unexpectedly won at Hurst Park racecourse on Saturday 14 September 1895, the *Sheffield Evening Telegraph* cursed "the luck of the Jews" explaining that "bookmakers of the Semitic persuasion – and there are many – [had] left Hurst Park to the Gentiles" and therefore been spared their share of the bookmaking losses.

Despite the exaggerated and racist tone of much of the criticism levelled against Jewish bookmakers it is clear, too, that some were engaged in illegal activity. Racecourse betting was dominated by criminal gangs for much of the early twentieth century, and this could occasionally spill over into violence and intimidation. One notorious Jewish group, called the Bessarabian Tigers, controlled gambling in the Whitechapel area of London's East End just before the First World War.

The Yiddishers were a London street gang led by Alfie Solomons, they opposed the growing fascist movement in Great Britain and participated in an attack on members of the British Union of Fascists known as the Battle of Cable Street in October 1936.

Joe Coral's betting shop on Regent Street, London

Another, headed by Alfie Solomons and his brother Harry, controlled north London and terrorised race courses around the country. Their violent feud with a rival Birmingham Irish gang was dramatized in the TV series *Peaky Blinders* (2013-present) where the character of Alfie Solomons was played by the actor Tom Hardy.

Real life Jewish involvement in nefarious gambling activities was gleefully seized upon by the British Union of Fascists in the 1930s to incite race hatred. In an echo of Nazi propaganda, fact and fiction were frequently mixed for incendiary effect, with publications such as *The Blackshirt* citing any examples of prosecutions against Jews involved in betting or race-course gangs as evidence of broader parasitic and debased characteristics. A typical piece in *Action* denounced Jewish bookmakers as having no interest in the sporting contest, arguing instead that "whenever large sums of money change hands ... there, battening like carrion on the pickings that may be found, are the most degraded specimens of an alien race".

Post-war reform of the gaming laws did much to clean up the image of all bookmakers – Jewish or otherwise. The Polish Jewish immigrant Joe Coral (born Joseph Kagarlitsky) was one of the first to recognise the potential of newly legalised off-course betting in 1960. Already an established betting operator at London's dog tracks, Coral moved his business to the high street, opening 23 betting shops by 1962. This figure had risen to 650 by the mid-1970s, making Coral one of Britain's leading firm of bookmakers. On his death in 1996 a spokesman for the Coral group told *Sporting Life* that "we will not see his like again", in tribute to Joe Coral's entrepreneurial flair.

Today Jewish participation in the 'Sport of Kings', whether as owners, bookmakers or spectators, is likely to go unremarked. Few would now regard possession of a thoroughbred stud as the key to social acceptance, although it may still have its advantages. Similarly, the antisemitic depiction of Jewish bookmakers as unreliable crooks, is as archaic and redundant as earlier representations of Jewish street hawkers. For a while, though, horse racing and its concomitant country pursuits was viewed as a means of social advancement for Jews and non-Jews alike. This was not always an easy journey, as the fictional Jewish socialite Ferdy Rabenstien discovered in *The Alien Corn* (W Somerset Maugham, 1931): "For many years he had followed hounds, but he was a bad rider and … it must have been a relief to him when he could persuade himself that middle age and pressure of business forced him to give up hunting. He had excellent shooting and gave grand parties for it, but he was a poor shot; and despite the course in his park he never succeeded in being more than an indifferent golfer. He knew only too well how much these things meant in England and his incapacity was a bitter disappointment to him".,

Alfie Solomons, portrayed by Tom Hardy in the BBC show *Peaky Blinders*, partnered with London Italian gangster Darby Sabini, also portrayed in the show, to control the North London rackets along with the race track activity of the day. Solomon, along with his brother Harry, also provided protection for Jewish bookmakers at the track.

'America's Number One
Goodwill Ambassadors"

Harlem Globetrotters' nickname

Biographies S – Z

Coached and owned by Abe Saperstein until his death in 1966, the Harlem Globetrotters are an exhibition basketball team. Founded by Saperstein in the late 1920s the Globetrotters became well known around the world, with stars such as Meadowlark Lemon, far left, appearing on tv shows such as the *Goldie Hawn Special*.

Harvey Sadow
Founder of Wingate F.C.

Major Harvey Sadow was one of the founders of Wingate Football Club. Alongside Maurice Rebak, Frank Davis, George Hyams and Asher Rebak, he created a Jewish club in an attempt to counter antisemitism. The team was named after Orde Wingate, the British army officer who had been involved in training the Haganah, a Jewish paramilitary organisation in the British Mandate of Palestine. Wingate F.C. did much to promote the idea of the "Sporting Jew" and give the lie to the notion of the "Jewish Weakling". The team began playing in the Middlesex Senior League, were founder members of the Parthenon League and were promoted to the Delphian, then Athenian Leagues. During their time in the latter the team represented Great Britain in the Maccabiah Games, often referred to as the "Jewish Olympics".

Abe Saperstein

Founder of the Harlem
Globetrotters
1902–1966

Abraham Michael Saperstein
was born in the East End of
London. His family originated
from Lomza in Poland. The
Sapersteins moved to Chicago
in 1907, settling in the city's
Jewish quarter. At the age of 10, young Abe discovered a love of
sport, playing basketball at the Wilson Avenue YMCA. He was
educated at Ravenswood Elementary School, Lake View High School
and the University of Illinois. Deciding not to follow his father into
tailoring, he created a basketball team known as the Chicago Reds.
He went on to become the booking agent for several basketball
teams, then formed one of his own in the late 1920s. He called the
team the New York Harlem Globetrotters. Although the team had
no connection with Harlem, Saperstein used the name to indicate
that his team was comprised of black players. Over the next few
years the team's reputation grew, with Saperstein himself subbing
in if a player was injured. In 1940 the Globetrotters beat the New
York Renaissance, and in 1948 came an even bigger coup – they
beat the Lakers, the best team in the all-white NBA. Saperstein
was a leading figure in black baseball leagues also. Originating
from a minority himself, Saperstein did much to showcase the
talents of the nation's best black basketball and baseball players.

Siegfried Sassoon
Poet and sportsman
1886–1967

The second of three sons, Siegfried Sassoon grew up in rural Kent. His heritage was from two very different lines – his father's Jewish family was born of the merchant princes of Baghdad, and his mother's family were originally farming stock from Cheshire. Sassoon abandoned a Cambridge education in favour of poetry, horses, cricket and golf. On the outbreak of the First World War he enlisted enthusiastically and served bravely, earning himself the Military Cross as well as the sobriquet "Mad Jack". The rest is poetic history – his injury at Arras in 1917, his shellshock, his convalescence at Craiglockhart hospital, which, due to the presence of fellow poet Wilfred Owen, turned into the most extraordinary literary salon. Although best known as a war poet, Sassoon was always a sporting man. His most famous novel, *Memoirs of a Fox-Hunting Man (1928)*, a humorous insight into a young man's initiation into that most British of blood sports, is widely believed to be autobiographical. At the onset of the First World War he remarked that "France was a lady, Russia was a bear, and performing in the county cricket team was much more important than either of them." His life's ambition was to play for Kent County Cricket Club, an ambition he never fulfilled. Other honours came his way, however: Sassoon was appointed CBE in 1951. Towards the end of his life Sassoon converted to Roman Catholicism.

Victor Sassoon
Racehorse owner
1881 - 1961

Ellice Victor Elias Sassoon was born in Naples, Italy to a Baghdadi Jewish family who were on the way to India. After such an eclectic start to his life his youth followed traditional British lines – he was raised in England and educated at Harrow school and Trinity College, Cambridge. He served in the Royal Flying Corps during the First World War and survived a plane crash in 1916. On the death of his father in 1924 he became 3rd Baronet of Bombay. He moved to India, then Shanghai, making a fortune as an hotelier. A fan of thoroughbred racing, Sassoon purchased the Bungalow Stud in 1925. Under Sassoon's trainer Sir Noel Murless, Sassoon enjoyed numerous victories for his horses at The Derby, Epsom and the St. Leger Stakes. Perhaps even more valuable, he was at the centre of the very cream of British Society. Sassoon was part of the establishment, describing himself as a 'Britisher'. He famously dismissed Hitler's rise as 'Bluff' referring to the dictator as merely 'H'.

United air crash victims was buried to-day. The cortege
ital for Southern Cemetery at Mr. William Satinoff's

Willie Satinoff
Businessman and superfan
1911–1958

William Satinoff was a Jewish businessman and fanatical supporter of Manchester United. He made his fortune in the cotton trade in the Manchester area. He was close to Matt Busby on a personal level, on the cusp of being elected to the club's board, when he was handed what seemed an amazing opportunity; to accompany the team he loved to Belgrade for the forthcoming European Cup Quarter Final tie as a representative of Manchester United Football Club. He never came back. Alongside the fabled "Busby Babes", he was killed when British European Airways flight 609 crashed on take-off at Munich-Riem Airport, on 6 February 1958. Although he was never formally commemorated by the club, Satinoff's grave, in Manchester's Jewish Cemetery, has become a place of pilgrimage for fans. The inscription reads: *To live in hearts we leave behind is not to die.*

Edgar Seligman
British fencer
1867 – 1958

Edgar Isaac Seligman was born in San Francisco in the United States. His father was Leopold Seligman. The family moved to London and Seligman became a naturalised British citizen. Seligman was a corporal in the Imperial Yeomanry and saw active service in the Boer War. He was a talented painter who exhibited at the Royal Academy. He found his greatest talent, for fencing, relatively late, at the age of 39, but he still managed to compete in four Olympic Games. In 1908, when England was the host country, Seligman made his Olympic debut at the age of 41. He then competed at Stockholm in 1912, Antwerp in 1920 and Paris in 1924. He won three consecutive team silver medals. He was also the only person to win the British title in each weapon he employed at least twice – with épée in 1904 and 1906, with foil in 1906 and 1907 and with sabre in 1923 and 1924. Seligman participated in two further Olympics, in 1928 and 1932, but in the art competitions.

Arnold Siegel
Football player

Arnold Siegel played for Leyton Orient. Like many Jews in the beautiful game, he faced the dilemma of what to do about playing on the Sabbath. Siegel was permitted to play on Saturday mornings only on the condition that he hid his football boots while he went to synagogue. His actions are emblematic of the necessary compromises made by many Jewish players and supporters; orthodox Jews had their season tickets sewn into their clothes to respect the law forbidding the carrying of items on the Sabbath.

Leslie Silver
Football chairman
1925–2014

Leslie Howard Silverstein was born in Walthamstow, London. When the garment factory his father worked in was bombed in 1940, the family moved to Leeds. Leslie followed his father into tailoring, but hated the profession. He volunteered for the RAF in 1943 and joined bomber command as a flight engineer. Returning to Leeds after the Second World War, Silver used his £250 demob money to set up the Silver Paint & Lacquer Company in 1947. The company manufactured thinners for the car industry, and by the time Silver retired in 1991 it had achieved sales of £100 million. Silver joined the board at Leeds United in 1981. He was chairman of the club from 1983 to 1996. When he took over, the team was struggling financially and plagued by hooliganism. Silver used his business acumen to rebuild the team's assets and presided over the sackings of managers Eddie Gray and Billy Bremner. He brought in Howard Wilkinson from Sheffield Wednesday and the team began to revive, winning promotion from the second to the first division. Wilkinson described Silver as the ideal chairman, "a guy of great humility, of great modesty and enormous integrity."

Alfie Solomon
Betting racketeer

Alfred "Alfie" Solomon was a gangster who worked out of Camden Town. Alongside his brother Harry Solomon, he ran the racetrack activity of the day. The brothers ran a protection racket for Jewish bookmakers at the track, and came to be both respected and feared. Solomon partnered with Italian gangster Darby Sabini, and stood trial for the attempted murder of Billy Kimber outside Sabini's house. Solomon was acquitted when all the eyewitnesses to the incident mysteriously and collectively lost their memory. In 1924 Solomon was once again charged with murder, this time of someone from the racing world. Bookmaker Buck Enden was killed in a fight when the Solomons demanded their racing debts. On this occasion there was no escaping justice for Solomon and he served three years' hard labour for his crime. According to a letter he wrote in 1930, Solomon claimed that: "Since being released I have got a respectable livelihood on the racecourses betting and have never been in trouble since and do not want to get into any." Solomon managed to stay out of trouble until recently, when his character was portrayed by Tom Hardy in the BBC's gangster drama *Peaky Blinders (2013–)*.

Harry Solomon
Betting racketeer

Harry Solomon partnered with his brother Alfie Solomon to control the Jewish bookmakers of England's racecourses. Operating out of Camden Town, the brothers ran a protection racket in return for a cut of the raceday winnings. Inevitably, the brothers ran into trouble with other gangs. They came to blows with rivals from Birmingham at Bath racecourse, in a standoff known as the *Battle of the Baths*. Harry was arrested for pulling a gun on a policeman.

Jack Solomons
Boxing promoter
1902–1979

Israel Jacob Solomons, known as Jack, was born in Petticoat Lane in the East End of London. He began his career promoting the Devonshire Club in Hackney in the 1930s, but the club was destroyed in the bombing of 1940. Solomons was forced to move his headquarters, and operated out of his gym in Great Windmill Street. His first high-profile fight was between Jack London and Bruce Woodcock for the British heavyweight title. In 1951 Solomons promoted the bout between Sugar Ray Robinson and Randolph Turpin, when Robinson famously lost his middleweight world title. Solomons promoted 26 world title fights in all, many of them at his favoured Harringay Arena in north London. Perhaps his greatest coup was the 1963 bout between Britain's Henry Cooper and the legendary Muhammad Ali. Jack Solomons was appointed OBE in 1978, and was inducted into the Boxing Hall of Fame in 1995.

Wilhelm Steinitz
Chess master
1836–1900

Wilhelm (later William) Steinitz was born in the Jewish ghetto in Prague, then in Bohemia (part of Austria) now in the Czech Republic. His father was a tailor, and Steinitz was the youngest of 13 sons. He learned to play chess at the age of 12. In his twenties he left Prague to study mathematics in Vienna, and began playing competitively. He improved rapidly, and earned himself the nickname "The Austrian Morphy" after American chess player Paul Charles Morphy. Success in the London Chess Tournament of 1862 led him to settle in the city. There he beat some of the UK's leading players including Augustus Mongredien and Frederic Deacon. He scored a significant win in 1866 against Adolf Anderssen, then considered the world's greatest player. Between 1873 and 1882 Steinitz took a break from competitive chess to concentrate on his work as a chess journalist, principally for *The Field*. He became engaged in an "Ink War" with Leopold Hoffer and fellow Jew Johannes Zukertort, who wrote for the rival publication *Chess Monthly*. Steinitz and Zukertort also had a fierce rivalry across the chessboard, battling for supremacy in the fabled 1883 London Chess Tournament. Losing narrowly to his nemesis, Steinitz decided to emigrate to the United States. In 1886 the rivals fought a return match on American soil, this time with Steinitz emerging as the victor. Seemingly unstoppable, Steinitz twice beat the legendary Mikhail Chigorin, but in 1894 he lost his world champion title to fellow Jew Emanuel Lasker.

Peter Taylor
Author of the Taylor Report
1930–1997

Peter Murray Taylor was born in Newcastle upon Tyne to a Yiddish-speaking Jewish family. The family's original name was Teiger or Teicher, and they hailed from Marjampole and Vilnius in Lithuania. Taylor was educated at the Royal Grammar School in Newcastle, then won a scholarship to read law at Pembroke College, Cambridge. He was called to the Bar in 1954 and "took silk" to become a Queen's Counsel in 1967. He took several high-profile cases, including prosecuting Stefan Kiszko and defending Jeremy Thorpe. But his connection to the world of sport began on 17 April 1989 when, as a high court judge in the Court of Appeal, he was commissioned by the government to lead an inquiry into the Hillsborough disaster that had occurred two days previously. A crush at the entrance to the Sheffield ground had claimed 96 lives, and Taylor's findings were published in the Taylor Report, on 29 January 1990. The report stated that all First and Second division stadiums had to be all-seater by August 1994. One of the most striking phrases of Taylor's report, given his heritage, was the description of spectators being treated like "prisoners of war". Since the report, no incidents even approaching the seriousness of Hillsborough have taken place.

Fred Trueman

Plain-speaking Yorkshireman
and cricketing genius
1931–2006

Fred Trueman was born
in Yorkshire, England. His
grandmother was Jewish.
Trueman started bowling at the
age of four and by eight had
made an appearance for his
father's club side. He attended Maltby Secondary School. Trueman
made his debut for Yorkshire against Cambridge in 1949, and two
years later he was awarded his county cap after some devastating
bowling against Nottinghamshire and Lincolnshire, including
his first hat-trick. 1952 saw Trueman make his England debut in
the series against India and he rose to the challenge, taking 29
wickets in the series. The following year Wisden named him as one
of their Cricketers of the Year. Owing to his tendency to fall out
with the cricket authorities, he did not become a mainstay of the
national side until 1957 when his formidable bowling partnership
with Brian Statham began. "Fiery Fred" went on to take 300 test
wickets, the first bowler ever to do so. Trueman only discovered
his Jewish origins in the 1990s but happily identified as a Jew. He
would often visit the opposition's dressing room before a match,
sometimes to see a friend but usually as "a declaration of war".

Sheila Van Damm

Theatre lover who became
one of Britain's most
successful rally drivers
1922–1987

Sheila Van Damm was born in
Paddington, London and raised
in a Jewish family. Van Damm
was a driver in the Women's
Auxiliary Air Force before training
as a pilot and joining the RAF after the Second World War. Her first
experience of motor racing was a marketing ploy for her father's
Windmill Theatre; she entered the MCC-Daily Express car rally in a
Rootes vehicle with "Windmill Girl" printed on the side and finished
in third place. Following her successful debut, the Rootes Group
invited her to join an all-women team for the 1951 Monte Carlo
rally. The next year, she won the ladies' prize in the Motor Cycling
Club rally and, in 1953, averaged 120 mph in a Sunbeam Alpine
to set the record for 2–3 litre cars and outpace Stirling Moss in
the process. Her partnership with Anne Hall saw the pair claim a
female victory – known as a coupe des dames – in many of the
toughest races including the 1953 Alpine Rally, the 1954 Tulip
Rally and, five years after her first attempt, the 1955 Monte Carlo
Rally. After a five-year stint in rally driving, Van Damm returned
home to the Windmill Theatre. She finished every race she started.

Victor Wahltuch
Chess master
1875-1953

Victor Wahltuch was born
in Chorlton-on-Medlock,
Lancashire. His parents were
Adolphe and Anna Wahltuch.
Adolphe was born in Odessa,
Ukraine, and became a licentiate
of the Royal College of
Physicians in London. Young Victor began playing chess at county
level and by the age of 30 represented Lancashire. In 1907 he
shared joint first with George Shories at Blackpool but won the
following year. In 1910 Frederick Yates was victorious, and Wahltuch
tied for 3rd-4th. After the First World War Wahltuch continued to
make his mark on the chess world. In 1921 he shared first place
with Yates in Manchester. He could manage no better than 13th-
14th in London in 1922, but his luck improved when he returned
to the north, taking 7th at Liverpool in 1923 behind victorious
fellow Jew Jacques Mieses. At the Hastings International Chess
Congress 1925/26 he came 8th, but moved up the rankings at
Scarborough where he managed 4th in 1927 and 1929. In 1931
Wahltuch played for England in the 4th Chess Olympiad in Prague.

Matt Wells
Boxer
1886–1953

Matthew "Matt" Wells was born
in Walworth, London. From
1905–7 he held the British
amateur lightweight crown,
and in 1908 he competed
in the Summer Olympics in
London. In his lightweight
event he lost in the quarter-finals to Frederick Grace, who went
on to win the gold medal. Wells turned professional in 1909. In
1911 he defeated Freddie Welsh to take home the Lonsdale belt.
He was the first Jew ever to achieve this feat. In the same year
he beat the great New York boxer and fellow Jew Leach Cross, at
the Harlem Casino. Wells was on a winning streak – on the same
Stateside trip he beat "Philadelphia" Pal Moore, "Knockout" Brown
and reigning world featherweight champion Abe Attell. In 1914
Wells won the Welterweight Championship of Britain and the
Welterweight Championship of the World. However, he only held
on to the world title for one year, losing to Mike Glover in Boston
Massachusetts. Wells's luck had seemingly run out – he lost to
Johnny Dundee and Charley White, and then failed to take the
welterweight championship from Johnny Basham in 1919. In the
same year he took a serious beating from fellow Jew Ted "Kid" Lewis.
Wells was inducted into the Jewish Sports Hall of Fame in 2007.

Baruch Wood

Eight-time winner of
the Warwickshire Chess
Championship
1909-1989

Baruch Harold Wood was
born in Sheffield, England. He
dominated the Warwickshire
chess championship for a
number of years, winning the
annual contest eight times. Wood's tournament record elsewhere
was very strong. In 1947, he won the Baarn tournament in 1954
at Paignton. Over the next 20 years, Wood placed first at Whitby,
Torshavn and Jersey. At the Hastings Christmas Chess Congress in
1948-49, Wood competed with the Russian Grandmaster Nicolas
Rossolimo, finishing just 1.5 points behind the champion. The
same year, Wood finished in tied second place at the British Chess
Championship in London. Wood also took the opportunity to
represent his country at the Buenos Aires Chess Olympiad in 1939.
He was a prolific writer on the game, and in 1935 founded the
popular *Chess* magazine, finally relinquishing control to Pergamon
Press in 1988. Wood also had a role as chess correspondent for
both the Daily Telegraph and the Illustrated London News. He
published his highly acclaimed Easy Guide to Chess in 1942. Wood
was the winner of the 1944-45 British correspondence chess
championship, a tournament conducted through the post.

Johannes Zukertort

Played in the first ever World Chess Championship match 1842-1888

Johannes Zukertort was born in Lublin, Congress Poland. His father was of Jewish origin but became a Protestant missionary. Since this was illegal in Russian-occupied Poland, the Zukertort family relocated to Prussia. Zukertort read medicine at the University of Breslau then served in the medical corps of the Germany army. He did not learn to play chess until the age of 19, and initially showed little promise. But after studying under Adolf Anderssen, one of the greatest ever players of the game, Zukertort's ability flourished and he defeated his teacher convincingly in 1871. Zukertort became a naturalised citizen of the United Kingdom in 1878 and there achieved his greatest career success, defeating the world's best players to win the London chess tournament in 1883. It was a victory that established him as contender to Wilhelm Steinitz in the battle for world champion, and the first ever World Chess Championship match was scheduled for 1886. Despite a strong start, Zukertort could not maintain the intensity and lost 12½-7½. It is said that three years prior to the showdown, Zukertort and Steinitz attended a dinner in which a toast was given to the future World Champion and both players stood up.

Harry Zussman
Football chairman

Harry Zussman was elected
chairman of Leyton Orient
Football Club in 1949, following
the death of former chairman
George Harris. It was a good
fit – Leyton Orient, or the
"Os" as they were known, had
a strong Jewish tradition. A
cherubic, cigar-smoking figure, described by Anthony Clavane as
an "East End fairy godfather", his first act was to appoint Alec Stock
as manager. He presided over the sale of record goal scorer Frank
Neary to Queen's Park Rangers for £7,000. The club lost to Torquay
in a thumping 7–1 defeat, but rallied in the newly launched Essex
Professional Cup, this time beating Clacton Town with the same
7–1 scoreline. Under Zussman the club were going in the right
direction, and in 1956 they gained promotion to Division Two for
the first time in their history, scoring a record 106 League goals.

"Go out on that stage and give it all you have got."

Sheila Van Damm

Photography credits